FROM TEE TO GREEN

FROM TEE TO GREEN

An Illustrated Anthology of
Classic Golf Writing

Dale Concannon

HEADLINE

For my father Austin,
the person who introduced me to this glorious game

First published in 1996
by HEADLINE BOOK PUBLISHING

10 9 8 7 6 5 4 3 2 1

Picture on previous page:
Giving nature a helping hand – sprinklers at Wentworth, 1993
(Allsport / Dave Cannon)

British Library Cataloguing in Publication Data
Concannon, Dale
From tee to green
1.Golf
I.Title796.3'52
ISBN 0-7472-1796-3

Typeset by Letterpart Limited, Reigate, Surrey
Printed and bound in Italy by Canale & C. Spa

HEADLINE BOOK PUBLISHING
A division of Hodder Headline PLC
338 Euston Road
London NW1 3BH

Contents

Part Three – Great Champions, Memorable Championships

Part Four – A Round of Golf

Introduction

Golf is a game which brings out the peculiarities and idiosyncrasies of human nature. It permits no compromises, recognises no weaknesses and punishes the foolhardy. Yet the apparent simplicity involved in hitting a small white ball from A to B lures all potential golfers into a false sense of security. Every instinct in the human psyche says the game looks easy, therefore it must be. That, for many of us, is where the trouble starts.

To play golf is the search for perfection. A seemingly endless struggle to attain the unattainable. It requires a complete mastery over emotion, nerve and temper with success or failure now depending on the individual's ability to handle all three at once. After all, in what other game are you expected to summon up the ability to drive a stationary ball with the force of a sledge-hammer one moment, then chip it with the delicate touch of a surgeon the next? Despite having the added benefit of no one else to hamper your progress, no other game offers so much potential for failure. Once taken up, golf must be treated with utter seriousness, otherwise the long-term effect could prove detrimental to both the mental and spiritual well-being of the individual.

So what makes the game so special? Certainly for those fortunate enough to have steered clear of its clutches, the devotion it inspires from its followers must appear quite absurd. The time, the effort, and amount of mental anguish expended on the sport, must seem wildly disproportionate to the actual pleasure it brings. No doubt most golfers would agree with this verdict. After all, who knows

'Putting' by William Laidlaw Purves, 1890. (Burlington Gallery)

what heights most of them could achieve, if but a small fraction of the energy and finance invested in the game was directed toward a more sensible goal?

Even for those who play it, golf remains an enigma. A strange mixture of frustration and joy, the game offers a limitless arena in which the full range of human emotions are displayed. The challenge of mastering the sport also appears to prove irresistible. For countless thousands each year, the sport becomes an obsession, with magazine articles detailing how to swing readily devoured and basic household chores neglected. It appears that once that first full-blooded drive has been smashed down the fairway, the golfing Rubicon has been well and truly crossed. You have joined the ranks of *Golfer Humanicus* where, in the words of Sir Walter Simpson:

> Nature loses her significance... Rain comes to be regarded solely in its relation to putting greens; the daisy is detested, botanical specimens are but hazards... Winds cease to be east, south, west or north. They are ahead, behind or sideways, and the sky is bright or dark according to the state of the game.

Over the years the challenge of explaining the root cause of this fascination has proved the golfing equivalent of finding the Holy Grail. As such, a vast body of writing has built up which far surpasses any other sport for sheer quantity. While many pieces have fallen by the wayside, others by comparison are wonderfully well written and occasionally breathtaking in their insight. Never presented in this format before, this illustrated golf anthology is a collection of some of the very best writings the sport has to offer. Designed to illuminate the golfing condition, it offers a unique insight into the very soul of golf. However, more of that later. First, let's do a little delving ourselves...

Perhaps, in terms that modern politicians like to employ, we should get back to basics. English Amateur Champion Robert Harris once described the workings of the game thus:

> A small ball has to be hit by a variety of clubs over grass country of uneven contour into a small hole in the ground. Difficulties in the shape of sand holes, ditches, streams, bushes and other natural objects are met in the journey from starting point to hole. These are surmounted by skilful shots or by-passed by manoeuvre. There are certain penalties and forfeits for inefficient play or an unlucky lie of the ball. These penalties have been exacted for centuries and found to operate with all fairness.

As a simple description of how the game is played, it cannot be faulted. Yet, as any golfer knows, the physical effort involved in hitting the ball from A to B is a relatively minor affair when taking in the game as a whole. Perhaps it is the challenge of improving one's own skill by one's own efforts, rather than having the comparative luxury of team-mates carry you along to success that makes the difference? Or, alternatively, a combination of the simple pleasures of life? Pleasures like being out in the open air, in attractive surroundings and enjoying the company of like-minded companions. Certainly golf is a mixture of all these elements, but then again so are many other sports.

Winston Churchill described golf as 'hitting a small ball into an even smaller hole, with weapons ill-designed for the purpose'. A frustrated golfer himself, who could deny his special insight into the eccentricities of the human race? But one question remains steadfastly unanswered. After resolving the world's ills, why did he not turn his attention to the most pressing question of the age: what is it about the game of golf that has such a profound effect on those who play it?

Just in case you thought golfing obsession was a fairly recent development of the human condition you would be mistaken. Back in the golfing dark ages, when the game was still in its infancy and Mother Nature was the only golf course architect, it had already started to weave its intoxicating spell. In 1593, two Scots named Pat Rogie and John Henrie were out playing on Leith Links near Edinburgh when they should have been attending Sunday Mass. With the game barely tolerated by Church authorities at the time, playing golf on the Sabbath had been strictly banned throughout Scotland over three decades before. Consequently, the two men were reported to the Town Burgess and forcibly dragged off the links.

After having their long-nose clubs and feathery balls confiscated, they were

'The Sabbath Breakers' by John Charles Dollman recreates the events of 1593. Even today, the Old Course at St Andrews remains closed for play on Sundays.

quickly brought for trial. Having been caught red-handed they faced three possible levels of punishment, with the first being a not insubstantial fine of two shillings. For repeat offenders, the next sentence was a spell in the municipal Seat of Repentance. This involved spending endless days locked into a stone chair situated in the local churchyard while local townspeople hurled copious amounts of rotting vegetables at you. Unfortunately for the two men, they were habitual golfers and third-time offenders. The punishment laid down by magistrates was both terrible and irreversible: for playing golf on the Sabbath, both men were to be jailed – then excommunicated!

Of course, this begs the question whether or not subjecting modern-day golfers to a small dose of hell-fire and damnation would do much good. Frankly, I have my doubts. What is certain is that, after spending over two centuries trying to ban the sport, the Scottish authorities finally gave up the ghost. Interestingly, though, golf is still banned on Sundays at St Andrews, with the rare exception of the Open Championship being held there. As for those two foolhardy golfers, their fate is unrecorded, but if I had to make an educated guess as to whether they stopped playing or not...

Another strange tale which illustrates the idiosyncratic nature of golf concerns a small group of British POWs incarcerated in Germany during the later part of the Second World War. After a year, one of them received a hickory shafted niblick with his Red Cross parcel and immediately set about hitting stones around the compound, much to the amusement of the camp guards. Shortly after, his fellow prisoners began feverishly manufacturing make-shift golf balls out of wool and string while others marked out a three-hole golf course. Occasionally, the Germans were called upon to retrieve the odd badly struck shot which had finished the wrong side of the electric fence, but for the most part all was relative harmony. Sadly, all this changed when one officer emphatically refused the chance to escape – it seemed he had planned an important golf match for the following day!

Not surprisingly, five centuries of golf history have thrown up countless other examples of this oddly obsessive behaviour. They include such notable examples as the man who bet his life on a game of golf – and lost; another who almost choked his partner to death over a dispute where the ball should have been placed on the green; the competitor who was prosecuted for throwing a live rattlesnake at his opponent in an attempt to put him off an important drive; or, indeed, the American golf pro who turned to robbing banks to supplement his lack of tournament earnings.

Quite what my purpose was in mentally recording such trivia I do not know. Perhaps it reflects the subconscious desire of all golfers to understand the quirky nature of the game that drives me on to acquire new and more bizarre stories. After all, in no other sport does the human mind play such an important role as it does in golf. In more physical games like tennis, the faster the rally the more instinctive it becomes but golf is a game which requires a great deal of thinking about. As early as 1910, American psychologist Arnold Haultain wrote, 'Most of the difficulties in golf are mental, not physical. Are subjective, not objective. Are the created phantasms of the mind, not the veritable realities of the course.'

In strictly literary terms, Haultain was not a typical golf author. His desire to explain the inner workings of the golfing soul was not born out of a deep love for the game, rather an overriding professional curiosity in the golfing neurotics who regularly visited his practice. Whether he achieved any practical success is uncertain, but his book – *The Mystery of Golf* – proved so popular with the golfing public at the time that it was re-published several times.

Despite admitting that he was a relative newcomer to the game, Arnold Haultain did make a valiant stab at explaining the inner meaning of golf. Then, after numerous chapters dealing with complex issues like the *Culpability of the Mind, Multiplicity of Consciousness and Psycho-physical Parallelism*, he finally admits, 'To sum up then, in what does the secret of golf lie? Not in one thing; but many. And in many so mysteriously conjoined, so incomprehensibly interwoven, as to baffle analysis.'

As Haultain's research proved, the writer's desire to explain the inner workings of the golfing soul can prove a frustrating task. Yet the search goes on in a variety of different ways. Despite the valid arguments put forward in his book, the majority of golf writers before and since have chosen a far less scientific route to explain the lure of golf. Some, like the great P. G. Wodehouse, chose humorous story-telling to express his thoughts on the game. Other respected writers on golf, like Horace Hutchinson, offered a more historical slant, while the classically educated Bernard Darwin preferred more descriptive prose. Whoever the author, no matter what aspect of golf they are writing about, each one reflects a deep and abiding fascination with the game through their work.

This anthology is the first book to address the reasons behind this all-consuming passion golfers have for their game. Illustrated throughout, it offers a wide-ranging mixture of items on different subjects, and offers an invaluable insight into the idiosyncratic nature of golf and those who play it.

The book itself is split into four main sections, each one dealing with a distinctive area of golf. The first is entitled *The Spirit of Golf* and details some of these various elements which have so fascinated golfers over the years. A medley of articles and extracts, comment and observation, it includes the work of such diverse writers as past British Prime Minister Arthur Balfour and the father of *Golfmanship*, Stephen Potter. The second, *A Royal and Very Ancient Game*, describes the early history and development of golf and some of the reasons why the game became so popular. Dramatic championships, classic golf courses and legendary champions of the past make up the section *Great Champions, Memorable Championships*. While the final chapter, *A Round of Golf*, is a potpourri of interesting and varied items dealing with, among others, women's golf, male attitudes towards women's golf, the art of caddying and comments on the future of golf itself.

When searching for likely material, it was decided from the very start to exclude nothing. All the way through, the greatest effort has been made to strike a good balance between the serious and the humorous, old favourites and the new. From the vast selection of short stories, magazine articles, biographies, historical items, memoirs, humour and travelogues on offer, the final choice depended on the quality of the work and its editorial relevance. Some will have been already published in this format before, many others will have not. In this desire to offer a golfing anthology which is both enjoyable, thought-provoking and above all fresh, I am proud to say this book contains items which have never been published before.

In keeping with the slightly nostalgic feel to the book, it was decided to make it an illustrated anthology by including photographs and illustrations which would complement the text. Offering a unique visual focus, each image has been chosen for its striking originality. Also in keeping with the theme of originality, a large majority of them are being published for the first time. A feat which was only possible with the help of numerous private golf collections, all of whose help I have gladly acknowledged.

Finally, one of the great pleasures of editing a golf anthology is the opportunity to re-read old favourites as well as making the acquaintance of many new ones. With so many wonderful writers to choose from, I still find the descriptive work of those like Bernard Darwin, Sir Walter Simpson and Garden G. Smith as fresh today as I did many years ago when first coming upon them in a local library. The same applies to the work of P. G. Wodehouse. I am certain that should I have been a member of his fictional Priors Wood Club in the 1930s, where the 'oldest member' spun his wonderful tales from the clubhouse terrace, I would have been far too enraptured to play golf.

For the record, though, my own personal favourite remains the early commentaries of Tobias Smollett. His descriptive narrative on those Gentleman Golfers of Leith in the mid-1700s shows what a fine line he must have drawn when chronicling the excesses of his betters. His subtle rebuke of their behaviour and how 'they never went to bed without having each the best part of a gallon of brandy in his belly' offers a glorious insight into how the game was enjoyed over two centuries ago.

Now, as I sit back and read it once more, those venerable old golfers with their whiskers and top-hats appear to come alive on the page. I can picture the look of eager anticipation as one of them tees up his feathery ball on a pinch of sand and sweeps it away down those ancient fairways. The glint of evening sun; the joyful chatter as they stride purposefully down the links attended by a small posse of scruffy caddies... Surely this was golf at its best.

This book celebrates that time and many others. With sparkling insights from some of the world's greatest golf writers, it offers a fascinating look into the unique nature of golf and those who play it.

PART ONE

THE SPIRIT
OF GOLF

Introduction

Golf is a curious game. It offers little of the heart-thumping excitement of sky diving, lacks the physical risk of shark fishing off the Tasmanian coast and pales into insignificance next to the naked fear induced by mixed doubles tennis. Yet as a devotee of the Royal and Ancient Game well knows, it has a certain something.

What it actually is we cannot be sure. However, any journey down the highways and byways of Britain during a winter blizzard will offer at least the faintest clue. As

A novel way of attracting business.
(Corbis UK Ltd)

the weary motorist ploughs his way through rush-hour motorway traffic, straining hard to see through the mini snowdrift which has built up on the windscreen, he need only glance sideways at a nearby field. There, standing frozen to their mashie-niblicks, will be a collection of golfers all impervious to the biting wind and freezing cold. A common enough sight, they can easily be distinguished by their hunched walk, ten layers of waterproof clothing and resolute look of determination. Of course should this vision excite a certain interest in the surprised motorist, it will not be because of the inclemency of the conditions. Rather, he is a golfer himself and envies others their opportunity for another round before nightfall...

Golf, it seems, furnishes its devotees with an intense, many-sided pleasure which few other forms of recreation can match. The game, simple in its fundamentals, is now played by millions worldwide who range in ability from expert to merely average and finally down to complete incompetent. It can be enjoyed alone in splendid isolation, or in small groups, depending on the circumstances and sociability of those involved. Basic equipment includes a ball, a club to hit it with, and enough free space to enjoy the results. Golf can be played from infancy to dotage, with a system of handicapping which enables the meanest duffer to compete on level terms with the finest of champions.

The ideal nature of the sport is, however, counter-balanced by the effect it has on those who play it. The first lesson the golfer learns is how much temperament and character play in the sport. With the game offering so much potential for personal embarrassment and failure, the individual quickly realises that the only *real* opponent in golf is yourself. Bad lies on well-mown fairways *are* the exception and not the rule; bunkers were not sited down the right-hand side just to capture the wicked slice you developed last week (or hook if you are left-handed). And trees have not spent the last two centuries growing to maturity solely with the intention of blocking your path to the green... Golf can prove an infuriating game for the unwary, but for a great many more it is coming to terms with this challenge that makes the game so exceptional.

This first section details that particular challenge. Offering an interesting and varied mixture of comment, history and superb golf writing, it illustrates the idiosyncratic nature of the game and those who play it. Including a selection of items dating back to the early days of golf in the 19th century, it reveals the challenging, often madly frustrating, qualities of the game. Including items by some of the finest golf writers ever known, like Horace Hutchinson and P.G. Wodehouse, it deals with everything from golfing temperament to the trials of winter golf. While many were written over a century ago, they all reflect the fascination golfers have with their sport and help explain just why golf is the game it is.

GOLF IS A REVEALER OF CHARACTER

Golf is a test of temper, a trial of honour, a revealer of character. It affords a chance to play the man and act the gentle man. It means going out into God's out-of-doors, getting close to nature, fresh air, exercise, a sweeping away of the mental cobwebs, genuine recreation of the tired issues. It is a cure for care – an antidote to worry. It includes companionship with friends, social intercourse, opportunities for courtesy, kindliness and generosity to an opponent. It promotes not only physical health but moral force.

David Robertson Forgan, 1898

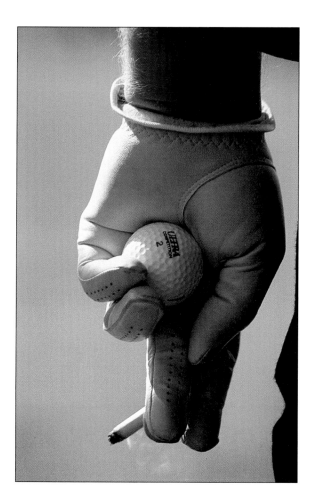

'Golf is ... a revealer of character.' The unmistakable hand of John 'Wild Thing' Daly.

THE MYSTERY OF GOLF

Three things there are as unfathomable as they are fascinating to the masculine mind: metaphysics, golf and the feminine heart. The Germans, I believe, pretend to have solved some of the riddles of the first, and the French to have unravelled some of the intricacies of the last; will someone tell us wherein lies the extraordinary fascination of golf?

Arnold Haultain, *The Mystery of Golf*, 1910

THE ART OF PUTTING

When a putter is waiting his turn to hole-out a putt of one or two feet in length, on which the match hangs at the last hole, it is of vital importance that he think of nothing. At this supreme moment he ought studiously to fill his mind with vacancy. He must not even allow himself the consolations of religion. He must not prepare himself to accept the gloomy face of his partner and the derisive delight of his adversaries with Christian resignation should he miss. He must not think that it is a putt he would not dream of missing at the beginning of the match, or, worse still, that he missed one like it in the middle. He ought to wait calm and stupid till it is his turn to play, wave back the inevitable boy who is sure to be standing behind his

'Silence is best' after holing a key putt. Ian Woosnam during his challenge for the 1989 US Open.

arm, and putt as I have told him how – neither with undue haste nor with exaggerated care. When the ball is down and the putter handed to the caddy, it is not well to say, 'I couldn't have missed it'. Silence is best. The pallid cheek and trembling lip belie such braggadocio.

Sir Walter Simpson, The Art of Golf, 1887

GOLF AND THE MAN

The boy, when he comes to the game, comes as an imitator: it is the easiest and best way to learn. It is a curious thing that when we grow older, though we have experience and knowledge, and even perhaps some philosophy to help us, we lose the power of imitation. How often have we seen the man of middle age in the agonies of a lesson, and utterly incapable of imitating the simplest movements of his instructor! 'Swing like this, sir,' says the professional; and his pupil answers, 'Ah, I see now.' But he can't do it, not he, and he will never do it, which is sad; and the whole scene would be pathetic were it not for the presence of the struggling learner's little son. He is standing behind, and when the teacher makes the imaginary swipes the boy bounds into the poise and rhythm of the movements in a moment. He will catch all the tricks and manners of a Sayers in half an hour, he will make the daisy-heads fly at every blow. But the father must learn with his head, and after many weary lessons, what the boy can learn with the eye in a few happy minutes. The chief danger of imitation is that we are too apt to imitate the extremes and not grasp the means wherein lies all the gold. It is the man who is too fat or too thin, or the one who has some strange gait or manner of address, who excites mimicry: the proper citizen does not attract our eye. And so in golf, the youth who comes to the game only as an imitator may never learn more than the attitudes and tricks; he may go on playing the monkey all his life. All through life man for the most part continues to be a learner of golf; many men even continue to take lessons till the end of their play. I remember only one man who was able to declare that he knew the whole theory and practice of the game perfectly, and he was a very bad player and a professor, which latter fact explains much; for professional golf is a thing quite apart. One has an idea that players who have been more or less self-taught are generally the best, and certainly the most interesting in their game. I do not mean that it is a bad thing to receive instruction; on the contrary, it is necessary that a man learn the principles, otherwise he will make no progress. But it is not a high ambition to be too long a pupil; every man, when he is perfect, is as his master; he has ceased to be a pupil, he has learned his lesson; the master is master of him no more, he himself has entered into the company of masters. Even though we never reach this high rank, we give up, after a time, receiving lessons except from ourselves; we try perhaps to work out some original stroke or to make ourselves masters of some manoeuvre which has lately brought us to grief. This is one of the ways in which man approaches the game with most chance of gaining at least pleasant entertainment. In the ordinary affairs of life we are so often saying and doing the things we have been taught to say and do, that we have a contempt for a golfer, who with all the licence of a game at his command, has no greater ambition than to copy the strokes of some expert. I once saw a man play golf like Vardon, and he played very well; but the performance irritated me, for I had seen the original. If the weather has been bad, and one has read two or three of the Reviews, how annoying it is to hear a pompous fellow at the back end of a dinner-party discoursing on our foreign policy and dishing the whole thing up, without even a fresh sauce, and placing it on the table as his original plate. We feel inclined to tell the man that we have read that morning's *Spectator*, and ask his opinion on the weather. In the same way with our copyist, we wish to ask him if he can do nothing of his own, if he cannot show us any sign that he has as a man tried to bring himself in contact with golf. We ask for originality, because whenever man by some fresh point of skill adds some new stroke to the play he raises once more both the player and the game. But without being copyists we may learn lessons from all kinds of tutors. The little boy who swings his over-heavy club 'right through', so that he finally lands on his head, is a good enough teacher, though we do not wish to emulate the whole of his performance. He has acquired what we call the 'follow-through', because he had no other choice once he had set his ponderous weapon in motion: he had no power to check the downward blow, he was under the control of the club, he had to go through with whatever the club felt inclined to do. Man, boasting himself, often fails because he cannot in his strength learn a simple lesson from a little child.

John L. Low, *The Royal & Ancient Game of Golf*, 1912

GENERAL REMARKS ON THE GAME

A fine day, a good match, and a clear green! These words sum up a golfer's dream of perfect happiness. How seldom is it fulfilled in this imperfect world of ours! He cannot command the weather. Wet is destructive to his clubs; and wind, if gusty, leads to wild driving and fills his eyes with tears when he tries to putt – a pitiable and humiliating condition. A clear green! No man can understand what land-hunger means until he has played, or tried to play, on a green which is too small for the number of players. Whatever his political views on other matters, he will at once become a rank socialist as to this, and call loudly for the compulsory allotment of those stretches of shore ground which are crying aloud to be converted into golfing greens. To make a good match, however, is to some extent in his own power; and he must be a weak or very good-natured man if he often

'A fine day, a good match, and a clear green! These words sum up a golfer's dream of perfect happiness' – the beautiful Valderrama Golf Club in Spain.

makes a bad one. But the match once made, let him make the best of his partner. And here is an opportunity for the study of character and the exercise of tact and self-control. Never scold; if your partner is timid, it will make him nervous; if obstinate, he will sulk; if choleric, he will say unpleasant things or break his clubs. If you praise, do so sparingly and judiciously and without seeming to patronise, or his pride may take alarm; and give as little advice as possible unless you are asked for it. It is wonderful how much can be got out of even a bad player by good management and good feeling.

Sir Walter Simpson, Golf, Badminton Library, 1890

THE COMMON SENSE OF GOLF

Out of a possible seventy-five millions (allowing for infants and infirm octogenarians), there are less than a million people in this country who play golf. At least seventy-four millions are wilfully depriving themselves of one of the most certain methods of attaining health and happiness. If you were assured that without imbibing any new-fangled religion and regardless of all the new dietists and doctors who fill the human body full of parasites for the sake of destroying other parasites, you could not only add twenty years to the normal span of life, but secure in the present at least one good day out of seven by the simple process of swinging a golf club, would you not rush to the nearest golf links and begin to take lessons from the local professional?

There really is no question about the results any more than there is doubt about

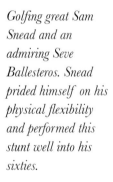

Golfing great Sam Snead and an admiring Seve Ballesteros. Snead prided himself on his physical flexibility and performed this stunt well into his sixties.

the pleasures of the game. Every other form of outdoor sport loses its votaries sooner or later. Baseball, football, riding, polo, even lawn tennis abandon us or we abandon them as our wind gets shorter and our bones more brittle. But once a golfer, you are wedded to the game for life. Nearly all the men who ever played golf and gave it up are those to whom athletic exercise in any shape is abhorrent. A few – perhaps even more than a few – have attempted to learn the game and have renounced it in disgust either because they could not see any fun in it or because they were such hopeless duffers that any sort of proficiency seemed out of the question.

These might well have been saved if they had only gone about it the right way. It is to these and to the many millions who have never even attempted to play that a few words of advice may be offered. If they will follow the advice given we guarantee health, sleep, immunity from nervous prostration and business worries, good temper, mental control, and lastly long life barring accidents from taxicabs or air ships. If those long-lived people who discovered for Professor Metchnikoff the virtues of the lactic acid had been nurtured on a golf links they would never have required germ tabloids to keep them alive.

It is easy enough to become a golfer if you happen to have been born in Scotland or even on Long Island; but how about the inhabitant of Keokuk or Kankakee, who has an equal right to liberty and happiness? When you come to think of it the wonder is not that so few people play golf, but that so many got along quite happily with such a bad imitation of the game. Most of our inland courses are so bad that to the uninitiated observer the game must appear a very futile kind of sport. In many cases the lies are abominable, the putting greens so coarse that no finesse in the short game is possible and in nearly all it is heavy odds that you cannot get round the links in summer without losing several balls.

H. J. Whigham, 1910

THE FOOZLE

While, on the whole, playing through the green is the part of the game most trying to the temper, putting is that most trying to the nerves. There is always hope that a bad drive may be redeemed by a fine approach shot, or that a 'foozle' with the brassy may be balanced by some brilliant performance with the iron. But when the stage of putting-out has been reached, no further illusions are possible – no place for repentance remains: to succeed in such a case is to win the hole; to fail, is to lose it. Moreover, it constantly happens that the decisive stroke has to be made precisely at a distance from the hole such that, while success is neither certain nor glorious, failure is not only disastrous but ignominious. A putt of a club's length which is to determine not merely the hole but the match will try the calmness even of an experienced performer, and many there are who have played golf all their lives whose pulse beats quicker when they have to play the stroke. No slave ever scanned the expression of a tyrannical master with half the miserable anxiety with which the performer surveys the ground over which the hole is to be approached. He looks at the hole from the ball, and he looks at the ball from the hole. No blade of grass, no scarcely perceptible inclination of the surface, escapes his critical inspection. He puts off the decisive moment as long, and perhaps longer, than he decently can. If he be a man who dreads responsibility, he asks the advice of his caddie, of his partner, and of his partner's caddie, so that the particular method in which he proposes to approach the hole represents not so much his own individual policy as the policy of a Cabinet. At last the stroke is made, and immediately all tongues are loosened. The slowly advancing ball is addressed in tones of menace or entreaty by the surrounding players. It is requested to go on or stop; to turn this way or that, as the respective interests of each party require. Nor is there anything more entertaining than seeing half a dozen faces bending over this little bit of moving gutta-percha which so remorselessly obeys the laws of dynamics, and pouring out on it threatenings and supplications not to be surpassed in apparent fervour by the devotions of any fetish worshippers in existence.

A. J. Balfour, *Golf*, Badminton Library, 1890

ETIQUETTE AND BEHAVIOUR

In a crowded state of the green, where the parties in front, however slow they be, are well up with the players in front of them again, all etiquette and custom requires that those in front should be allowed to travel well out of range before the legitimate privilege of the players behind, to drive after them, be exercised. We say in a crowded state of the green, and when the parties in front are well up with those again in front of them; for when this is not the case, when a certain slow-going match has a free space of a hole's length, or more, before them, when they are retarding the progress of all behind, then etiquette does not prescribe any such forbearance. The requirements of etiquette then fall upon the slow-coaches – that they shall allow the faster-going singles or foursomes to pass them by. Otherwise they have no just ground for complaint if they find the tee-shots of those behind them whizzing past their ears, after they have played their seconds, in such wise that they will probably deem it the part of prudence, no less than of courtesy, to let their swifter pursuers go before them. Yet the pursuers should in this case reflect that this concession is an act of courtesy, and accept it with due thanks.

In no case and under no circumstances save where a ball is lost, and permission obtained, is it excusable to drive into a party along the green, on the putting-green, or before they have played their seconds. Where the parties behind have infringed this great commandment more than once during a round, any means combining

Two golfing legends, Arnold Palmer and Gary Player, in conversation on the Turnberry links during the 1990 Seniors' Open.

an insistence upon your rights with adequate courtesy of the offenders is beyond our ingenuity to suggest; but it may perhaps be urged that players thus offending have forfeited all claim to courteous dealing.

There is a certain point in regard to match play which has been the cause of considerable exasperation, upon occasions. It occurs more often, perhaps, than elsewhere upon the links of St Andrews, where caddies, greens, and winds are keen. There the canny caddie upon a windy day will station himself at the hole in such manner as to shield the wind off the ball of the master for whom he carries. Not content with that, he will shuffle after it as it is propelled by the wind and with feet close together coax it, so far as possible, to travel in the way it should go, with all the art of a curler. Should the ball be over-strongly putted, and the wind be opposed to its course, he will jump aside to allow the full current to blow against it. This can, of course, be only done by the caddie who is standing at the hole. There occurs often, therefore, some competition between the rival caddies as to which shall have this post. There results discussion, and some unpleasantness. Now the proper etiquette is that the caddie of him whose turn it is not to play should stand at the hole; for it is in the interest of the non-player that the caddie, who can move aside, stands at the hole in lieu of the flag-stick, which the player might gain an advantage by striking. If this rule then be adhered to, there can be no opportunity for the caddie thus 'favouring' the ball; for even the least scrupulous of them do not go the length of attempting to turn the wind to the disadvantage of the ball of their master's antagonist. And as for this shielding of the wind off the ball, we would say that it is altogether opposed to the true spirit of the game, which consists in the combining of skill of hand with calculation of just such conditions of wind, &c., as this virtually unfair conspiracy between master and caddie tends to modify. In the abstract we believe that all gentlemen condemn the practice, though in actual course of play, partly from a dislike to check the zeal shown by the caddie in their interests, they often permit it without rebuke.

The relations between partners in foursomes are governed entirely by a tacit code of etiquette. The better player should be on his guard against any show of patronage in his advice; the inferior partner should show proper contrition for his misdoings, but should not be in a continual state of apology as if a mistake was with him an exception. The amount of conversation between partners should be determined by the inclination of him who wishes to talk least. The prior claim is that of the negative blessing of silence; and this is true no less in your partnership with another in a foursome than in regard to your relations with an opponent in a match.

More especially is it incumbent upon spectators to preserve silence and immobility, and it is in the worst taste for them to come forward and offer unsolicited and probably unwelcome conversation with any of the players in the intervals of the strokes. Spectators should always remember what is due to those who are affording the spectacle; but it is no less true that a duty of courtesy is owed by the players to those who pay them the compliment of being interested in their performance. Moreover, golf links are commonly public places. The spectator has as good a right there as the most finished golfer, and the latter should not forget that if the former defer to the delicate requirements of his nervous system, it is but an act of courtesy, and should be received with the courteous acknowledgment due to such.

Modesty is a virtue, but the mock modesty, the pride which apes humility, was an occasion of much mirth to Satan; and it is a breach, rather than an observance, of etiquette, and even of honesty, to so underrate your game as to gain an unfair advantage in arranging the conditions of a match. Do not tell a player whom you have defeated that he would be sure to beat you next time. He may think so, but he will not believe that you do, and the remark partakes of the nature of an insult to his understanding.

Finally, there are certain points of etiquette, such as those connected with dress, which differ, locally, and you should ever endeavour to conform yourself to the etiquette of the links on which you may be playing. Thus, on some links it is especially requested, as a means of warning the public of the approach of danger, that the golfers should wear red coats. It is but fair towards the local members of the club whose guest or visiting member you temporarily are that you should array yourself for the nonce in the uniform of the danger-signal. Otherwise, any damage inflicted on the unwary passer-by by your approach unheralded save by the hard flying golf-ball will be laid at the innocent door of the club, to the injury, in the opinion of the vulgar, of its local habitués.

Horace Hutchinson, Golf, Badminton Library, 1890

THE EIGHT-INCH GOLF COURSE

Establishing the Proper Mental Patterns
Every game of golf that has ever been played – whether the medal was 68 or 168 – has taken place on a golf course that measured eight inches more or less. I arrived at the dimensions of this golf course by taking a ruler and measuring my own head from back to front. Of course, every game of golf is played – every shot is played – in your mind before the ball actually starts on its way.

You've heard before about golf being a mental game. So have I. But my objections to most articles on the mental side of golf have been that the nut or kernel of the message seems to be that the mental side is vital, but then what?

If a woman wants to cut a dress – if a foundry wants to make a casting – if an architect starts to design a building – the basis of the finished product is a plan or pattern. The finished product, properly erected, is an exact reflection of the original plan or pattern.

If you wanted to learn a verse – wanted to learn to speak it effectively – you would commit it to memory, with every inflection and emphasis necessary to make a good delivery. This would be your 'pattern'. And – when you wanted to deliver the verse – mentally you'd fish out your pattern and go ahead – practically the same every time, gaining skill, ease and certainty with repetition.

It is exactly the same thing with the game of golf – every shot, successful or otherwise, is the result of a mental pattern. Of course, in speaking the verse, your voice is the vehicle through which the pattern is reproduced. And your voice is more or less easily controlled. On the other hand, the mental patterns used in the golf shot express themselves through many, many muscles.

So, the patterns – the *right* patterns – must be slowly and painstakingly built up.

The mental game of golf, as demonstrated by Seve Ballesteros during the 1996 Dubai Desert Classic.

Their part is so impressed upon your 'muscular memory' that their execution requires no conscious thought.

The mental patterns of the professional are so set that when he steps up to his ball, his only conscious thought should be where he wants it to go, and then the decision to send it there. Ask any professional you know if he carries any thought besides these after he has decided upon the playing of his shot.

The stance must be built upon a mental pattern. When that pattern is developed, you are able to step up to your ball and – without conscious thought – know where the ball is going as the result of the position you assume in relation to it.

The 'grip' of the club is the subject of another mental pattern. When you have the right mental pattern of your grip, you know that the face of the club is not going to turn over or turn up when it comes to the ball; it's fair, square and true.

The arc of your swing, the timing, the feel of the clubhead – all of these things are basic mental patterns which find execution through your muscular memory.

In the putt – short or long – direction is simpler to visualise than distance. Thus, the better the mental pattern of the proper force of the blow, the closer the ball comes to the cup.

I know this *sounds* complicated. I don't believe that, once understood, it will be so, however. On the contrary, I firmly believe that it is the greatest step possible toward simplification of golf instruction.

Eddie Loos, *The American Golfer* magazine, October 1924

THE GREAT SECRET

When he reads of the notable doings of famous golfers, the eighteen-handicap man has no envy in his heart. For by this time he has discovered the great secret of golf. Before he began to play he wondered wherein lay the fascination of it; now he knows. Golf is so popular simply because it is the best game in the world at which to be bad.

'The best game in the world at which to be bad' – provided there is someone to retrieve your mishit shots.

Consider what it is to be bad at cricket. You have bought a new bat, perfect in balance; a new pair of pads, white as driven snow; gloves of the very latest design. Do they let you use them? No. After one ball, in the negotiation of which neither your bat, nor your pads, nor your gloves came into play, they send you back into the pavilion to spend the rest of the afternoon listening to fatuous old stories of some old gentleman who knew Fuller Pilch. And when your side takes the field, where are you? Probably at long leg both ends, exposed to the public gaze as the worst fieldsman in London. How devastating are your emotions. Remorse, anger, mortification, fill your heart; above all, envy – envy of the lucky immortals who disport themselves on the green level of Lord's.

Consider what it is to be bad at lawn tennis. True, you are allowed to hold on to your new racket all through the game, but how often are you allowed to employ it usefully? How often does your partner cry 'Mine!' and bundle you out of the way? You may spend the full eighty minutes in your new boots, but your relations with the ball will be distant. They do not give you a ball to yourself at football.

But how different a game is golf. At golf it is the bad player who gets the most strokes. However good his opponent, the bad player has the right to play out each hole to the end; he will get more than his share of the game. He need have no fears that his new driver will not be employed. He will have as many swings with it as the scratch man; more, if he misses the ball altogether upon one or two tees. If he buys a new niblick he is certain to get fun out of it on the very first day.

And, above all, there is this to be said for golfing mediocrity – the bad player can make the strokes of the good player. The poor cricketer has perhaps never made fifty in his life; as soon as he stands at the wickets he knows that he is not going to make fifty today. But the eighteen-handicap man has some time or other played every hole on the course to perfection. He has driven a ball 250 yards; he has made superb approaches; he has run down the long putt. Any of these things may suddenly happen to him again. And therefore it is not his fate to have to sit in the club smoking-room after his second round and listen to the wonderful deeds of others. He can join in too. He can say with perfect truth, 'I once carried the ditch at the fourth with my second', or 'I remember when I drove into the bunker guarding the eighth green', or even 'I did a three at the eleventh this afternoon' – bogey being five. But if the bad cricketer says, 'I remember when I took a century in forty minutes off Lockwood and Richardson', he is nothing but a liar.

For these and other reasons golf is the best game in the world for the bad player. And sometimes I am tempted to go further and say that it is a better game for the bad player than for the good player. The joy of driving a ball straight after a week of slicing, the joy of putting a mashie shot dead, the joy of even a moderate stroke with a brassie; best of all, the joy of the perfect cleek shot – these things the good player will never know. Every stroke we bad players make we make in hope. It is never so bad but it might have been worse; it is never so bad but we are confident of doing better next time. And if the next stroke is good, what happiness fills our soul. How eagerly we tell ourselves that in a little while all our strokes will be as good.

What does Vardon know of this? If he does a five hole in four he blames himself that he did not do it in three; if he does it in five he is miserable. He will never experience that happy surprise with which we hail our best strokes. Only his bad strokes surprise him, and then we may suppose that he is not happy. His length and accuracy are mechanical; they are not the result, as so often in our case, of some suddenly applied maxim or some suddenly discovered innovation. The only thing which can vary in his game is his putting, and putting is not golf but croquet.

But of course we, too, are going to be as good as Vardon one day. We are only postponing the day because meanwhile it is too pleasant to be bad. And it is part of the charm of being bad at golf that in a moment, in a single night, we may become good. If the bad cricketer said to a good cricketer, 'What am I doing wrong?' the only possible answer would be, 'Nothing particular, except that you can't play cricket.' But if you or I were to say to our scratch friend, 'What am I doing wrong?' he would reply at once, 'Moving the head' or 'Dropping the right knee' or 'Not getting the wrists in soon enough', and by tomorrow we should be different players. Upon such a little depends, or seems to the eighteen-handicapper to depend, excellence in golf.

And so, perfectly happy in our present badness and perfectly confident of our future goodness, we long-handicap men remain. Perhaps it would be pleasanter to be a little more certain of getting the ball safely off the first tee; perhaps at the fourteenth hole, where there is a right of way and the public encroach, we should like to feel that we have done with topping; perhaps –

Well, perhaps we might get our handicap down to fifteen this summer. But no lower; certainly no lower.

A. A. Milne, *Not that it Matters*, 1919

STRANGE OPPONENTS AND PARTNERS

I have met strange opponents at golf; even stranger partners. I was once paired with an elderly man, till then unknown to me, now for ever memorable, who, after informing me, in confidence, that he was a familiar figure at St Andrews in the gutta-percha days, missed the object on the first tee, and, before I could intervene, took a second swish at the ball, which hit the ladies' tee-box and rebounded behind us into a gorse-bush. By weird methods we reached the sixth tee, which is high up, with a valley on each side. Off this he fell, to the left, while explaining the grandeurs of the hole, and we became a three-ball match.

I have played in a two-ball sixsome, on the same side as an Irish Protestant parson from Cork and an average-adjuster – a profession, surely, of magnificent

vagueness to the uninitiated. I cannot recollect who won. At Lindrick, that lovely course on the borders of three counties, I have partaken in a one-hole, one-club match with fourteen others, on a summer's evening, and the heavens were darkened with balls, as was the sun, so they say, with arrows at Marathon!

But the strangest man I ever knew on the links was a regular opponent, of middle age and middle handicap. At once let it be remembered that he was a man of kindliest character, which he hid beneath fierce austerity of look and a power of invective that were matchless in their time. His clubs seemed for ever to be on the verge of total collapse; there was a driver from which string and plaster flapped protestingly; a mongrel mid-iron, withered and rusty, with which he played what he was pleased to call his 'push-shot'; a putter that was wry-necked and, though, I suppose, within the law, yet against equity and nature.

He would arrive, with erratic, curse-these-golf-club-garages swerves, on to the scene, give me a passing glare, disappear into the dressing-room, from which emerged sounds like a boot-fight between customer and assistant on a sale-day, then dash to the first tee. Then he would allow me a curt nod of recognition, and shout such single comments as 'Off as soon as possible – late – course overcrowded – too many women – shouldn't play at all – talk to the secretary.' I have, indeed, known him to tee his ball in front of three waiting pairs, drive it off, and expect me to do the same. In others this would be accounted rude; in him it was natural, even magnificent.

As to his language during the hours of play, I have often thought that I missed the best; for he had known me since I was very young; sometimes, however, when he had sliced into a bunker (designed by the devil and executed by a brutish green

Greg Norman, 'the convenient invalid', enjoying some light relief with Jack Nicklaus during the World Match Play event at Wentworth.

committee), he would be heard to choke back some tremendous oath, composed of many moods and adjectives; and the word would roll back, stillborn, into the furnace of his frame! He regarded those playing around him as natural enemies and idiots, and once, when he missed a very short putt, he yelled down an adjoining fairway: 'D–n you, sir! Do you mind not flashing your brassy like that while I am putting?' On the tees during his practice swings the herbaceous vandalism was frightful to see; but, as the fids of turf spurted into the air, his comment would be: 'Club much too long – can't make it out,' or: 'Dropping the right shoulder again.'

Yet I have given, could only give, a faint and ghostly picture of this terrific golfer. Again, on a handicap of fourteen, a figure which facetious members would remark he had decided upon himself, as a Napoleonic committee of one, he was no mean opponent. I can see him now, at the end of the game, still in a fierce hurry, cranking up and maledicting his obsolete car, which he drove, on his more careless days, as wildly as his golf ball, perchance sweeping away in transit a tradesman's bicycle, and sending hens jittering and flapping through the hedges!

Of all types of opponent the most irritating is, I think, 'the convenient invalid', that self-pitying monster whose hooks are the result of some galloping and mortal disease, who cannot putt because of hay-fever, who tops his mashies owing to synovitis in the elbow, is only playing because of medical advice, yet will, in fact, only reach his true form on the plains of Elysium, or elsewhere. I once knew such a fellow rudely cut short by a military opponent, who bawled at him: 'D–n, sir; if I had your blasted lumbago, I could control my infernal swing, sir!'

Then there are those opponents who say 'Bad luck' when you miss from eighteen inches, others who remark: 'Funny, I thought you'd carried that bunker for certain,' or: 'Didn't think you'd miss that one, as my ball was giving you the line.' These, surely, must have their appointed after-life.

Less trying, but somewhat embarrassing, are those who say nothing at all, till suddenly, about the eleventh tee, they snap out 'One up' or 'Three down.' Others there are who, when you are four down at the turn, and there are five couples waiting to drive off on a bleak day, begin with that dispiriting sentence: 'Last time I played this hole...' and, I am afraid, we wish darkly that this could be the last time that he could play *any* hole. Ah! What bitter men are we golfers! How selfish in our thoughts! How petty in our little strifes! Day after day we wage our insignificant battles, curse our fate, as we smile with wan politeness; loathe our beastly opponent, his wretched, sniffing caddie, and his intolerable new set of irons. Grant me, when all is said, an old and forthright friend to play against, who swears and laughs at his own strokes and yours, likes to see you in a bunker and says so, seldom cries 'Good shot!' but, when he does, means it; takes golf as one of the world's eternal and necessary humours – and has a comfortable car!

R. C. Robertson-Glasgow, *Morning Post*

GOLF GAMESMANSHIP

The Drive
Of all the problems which face the golf gamesman, the problem of pure good play is the most difficult to fight. In particular, some of the best gamesmanship brains in America, many of them drained from England which drained them from Scotland, have been bent to the problem of how to be one-up on the man who hits the longer ball.

In normal circumstances it may be possible, for instance, to give advice to a man who is 2 or 3 up: but it is difficult indeed if he is outdriving you. A list of attempted ploys looks little better than a confession of failure. There is the driver from the head of which you unbutton a head cover marked with a large 'No. 4'. There is the remark, if your own drive of 150 yards happens just to have cleared the rough on the right, that 'position is the point here, not distance'.

Then there is the old ploy, first mentioned by me in 1947, of giving your Vast Distances man a caddy who never says 'good shot' but often points to a place, 30 yards ahead, which was reached by Byron Nelson when he played the course in 1946, or, better still, by J. H. Taylor, when he played there with a gutty in '98.

The problem will be solved in time. Funds for our Long Ball Research Wing are welcome and needed. Meanwhile let me give one piece of general advice. Never, never comment on the fact that your opponent has got distance. Never say 'You

Legendary clown Harpo Marx and Sam Snead share a joke at the 1972 Bob Hope Pro-Am Tournament at Pebble Beach, California.

certainly powdered that one'. Puzzled by your silence, long driver will try to outdistance even himself until, inevitably, he ends up out of bounds.

But the important point to remember is that superiority in length is a myth, or is at any rate cancelled out by relativity. It depends on the standard of measurement. The man who is outdriven at Sandwich can always say 'when Sarazen won here he never used more than a 3 wood'. A following breeze may help you to make the 200 yard mark down wind at the 18th at St Andrew's. But if your opponent beats you by his usual fifteen yards it is usually safe to say:

'Amazing to think that in these conditions Nicklaus *reached the green* in all four rounds of the Open.'

Safe unless you are up against a St Andrew's type gamesman who will probably say:

'Yes. I wonder what club he used from the tee. After all, two generations ago Blackwell reached the *steps leading up to the clubhouse* with a gutty.'

It might be added here that the inferior player should never, never in any way behave differently, let alone apologise, because he is inferior. In the days when I was genuinely young and had muscles like whipcord I used to drive nearly 210 yards on the downhill hole at Redhill. My father's best was 140 yards. As soon as he had struck one of these hundred-and-forty-yarders, he would stand stock still gazing after the ball till it had stopped and then pace the distance, counting out loud, and ending in a crescendo 'a hundred and thirty-eight, *thirty-nine*, FORTY'.

It is worth noting here that if Long Handicap is playing Short – 14 playing 4, for instance – never must 14, if he wins, admit, recall, apologise or refer in any way to the fact that he has received 8 strokes in the round; and it is most unusual to refer to this when telling the story to family, particularly wife. This situation and its handling show yet once again the deep relationship between life and golf, of which life is so often the metaphor or mime.

Style

This is the place to say something not about the style of gamesmanship but the gamesmanship of style. A perfect, flowing, model style can be alarming to an opponent. The teaching of golf is not our domain: but the teaching of style comes very much into our orbit. An appearance of a strong effortless style, flowing yet built on a stable foundation, can be alarming to an opponent even if it has no effect on one's shots.

'Right, let's have a game then,' says Jeremy Cardew to comparative stranger after a dinner party.

'I haven't played for ages,' he goes on. Though in full evening dress, he may pluck a bamboo stick from a pot in the conservatory and begin to take a practice swing, left hand only.

'My, what a wide arc to that swing,' thinks Wiffley, who is already wondering if he, too, ought to have worn a white tie instead of a black. We recommend the suggestion of great width, on this back-swing, and long relaxed follow-through.

Above all we recommend practising a practice swing which ends with the body turned correctly square to the direction of the ball, the hands held high, an expression of easy confidence on the face, a touch of nobility, as if one were looking towards the setting sun. Students who find themselves unable even vaguely to simulate a graceful finish may do well by going to the opposite extreme. It is possible to let go of the club almost completely at the top of the swing, recover it, and by a sort of half-paralysed jerk come down again more or less normally. Opponent will find himself *forced to stare at you*, and may lose his rhythm.

Straight Left Arm: A Personal Confession

I am sometimes asked which, of all the gambits I have invented, do I personally find most useful. Here, exclusively and for the first time, let me reveal the answer to this question.

In golf I have no doubt. Described in Gamesmanship, it is for use against the man who is driving farther and less erratically than yourself.

'I see how you're doing it,' you say, 'straight left arm at the moment of impact, isn't it? Do you mind if I stand just here and watch?'

In spite of the fact that the left arm is always straight at the moment of impact, this used to cause a pull in the old days. Now there is a well-developed counter. But in '68 I am still finding it useful.

Stephen Potter, The Complete Golf Gamesmanship, 1968

GOLF IN THE OLD COUNTRY

To the occasional or casual observer there appears in the Englishman's demeanour on the links no departure from his usual placidity. He stalks upon the grounds with habitual solemnity, and takes up the game in the same seriousness that has been associated with him at play. If the on-looker follows the player around the course,

The most famous sight in golf: the imposing stone clubhouse of the Royal and Ancient Golf Club of St Andrews.

he seeks in vain for any visible sign of that joyous spirit which he, likely as not, has imagined fitting accompaniment to athletic contest.

But in golf the Briton is a contradiction. He gives no outward evidence of perturbation, though, to borrow topical opera slang, he boils within. It is only to his familiars in the club-house and around his own board that the Englishman reveals himself, and there, by the softening influences of good cheer, may you discover how hopeless a victim he is to the ancient and royal game.

Before he has finished his Scotch and soda he will play over again every stroke of that last round in which he was beaten a single hole, and then take up in elaborate detail certainly every bunker and almost every brae on the course, until he has at length decided to his complete satisfaction on the identical stroke and spot that caused his downfall. I should be willing to give long odds in a wager on every golfing enthusiast in Great Britain being able to find, blindfolded, any given hazard on his home links, and the great majority of hazards on every course in England or Scotland. To hear them discuss strokes to evade, I was near saying, almost every bit of whin, and locate every sand dune is to gain some idea of the range and strength of golf mania.

I was prepared to find the country gone golf-crazy, but I found instead a condition bordering on what I have called golf-insomnia, though I should add that my observations were made from esoteric vantage-ground. At first I was disappointed, and ascribed the stories I had heard of the golf-furor to newspaper licence; I had looked for some familiar token by which I might recognise the craze – signs such as in America indicate unmistakably that a boom is on. But my first visit to links so depressed me that I nearly reached a determination to pass by golf altogether in my pilgrimage – in the eventual failure of which resolution my readers have my heart-felt sympathy.

It was a disillusioning experience, that first sight of the much-heralded and antique game. Speaking retrospectively, I am not sure I have a very distinct recollection of just what I reckoned on viewing; I do not believe I expected to see players astride their clubs prancing about the teeing-ground in ill-concealed eagerness for the affray, nor a dense and cheering throng of spectators surrounding the putting-green of the home hole, nor triumphantly shouldered victors borne from the field amid hosannas and tumultuous applause by the populace.

Even as I write now I can feel again the dejection that came over me in successive and widening waves as I looked for the first time on the game that is reported to have converted in the last two or three years more disciples than any other in the old country. At first I thought I had gone on the links during a lull in the play. Then I persuaded myself that I had arrived on a day set apart from the convalescents of some near-by sanitarium, but as I discovered my error in the ruddy imprint of health on their cheeks, my wonder grew that so many vigorous, young, and middle-aged men could find amusement in what appeared to me to a melancholy and systematised 'constitutional'.

Once recovered from the initial shock, I found amusement in the awful solemnity that enveloped the on-lookers about the putting-green, every mother's son of whom watched the holing out with bated breath. One, standing next to me in the crowd, and whose pleasing face gave encouragement, while the frequency with which he had trod on my toes seemed to me to have established a sufficient *entente cordiale* between us, bestowed upon me, when I asked why no one called the number of strokes each player had taken, so we would all know how they stood, such a look of righteous horror as I am sure would have caused any but an irrepressible American to wish the earth might open and swallow him. But being an American it simply increased my thirst for knowledge, and at the next sally I upset him completely by asking why a player, who was executing the 'waggle' with all the deliberate nicety of one thoroughly appreciative of that important prelude to the flight of the ball, did not hit it instead of wasting so much time and energy flourishing his 'stick' above it.

To have alluded with levity to one of the rudimentary functions of the game was appalling enough in all conscience, but to have called a club a stick was too much for my neighbour, and he of the aggressive feet moved away from the tee with a pained expression clouding the open countenance that had tempted my golfing innocence.

Subsequent and solitary wanderings about the links brought but little solace to my joyless sporting soul, for it seemed that at every turning I was challenged by loud and emphatic cries of 'fore', the significance of which I did not understand, while the air appeared to be filled with flying balls that whizzed past at uncomfortable proximity, or alighted just behind me, after a flight of a hundred and fifty yards or so, with a thud far from reassuring. It does not seem probable such a situation could under any circumstances have a humorous side; but it may, and I have laughed until my head ached over the comical consternation of some luckless and obstinate duffer, who, instead of permitting, as courtesy and tradition teach, more skilful following players to pass him, continued on his laborious and turf-bruising way, driven into by those immediately back of him, and damned by every golfer on the links. Given an irascible and stubborn and indifferent (a combination that has been known to exist) leading player, with following balls dropping around him, and I fancy even an Englishman, if he is not playing, will acknowledge the picture mirth-provoking.

What broke the gloom of that first day of my experience, and turned indifference to a desire for knowledge, were the individual manoeuvres on the putting-green, which, sometimes grotesque, frequently picturesque, and invariably fraught with the weightiest meditation, convinced me that any game requiring such earnest play must improve on acquaintance. The putting-green presents a scene for the student of human nature, with its exhibitions of temperaments and varied styles of play: one will make a minute and lengthy survey over the few yards of turf that separate his ball from the hole, and attain the climax of his joy or woe by a short sharp tap with the club; another devotes his critical attention to the lie of the ball, followed by a painfully deliberate aim that seems never to quite reach the explosive point; some appear to acquire confidence by the narrowing of the human circle around the hole; others wave all back save their caddie, who, like a father confessor, remains at their side administering unction of more or less extremity to the last.

The duties of the caddie are manifold, including the responsibilities of preceptor, doctor, and lawyer. He will be called upon to devise means of escape from soul-trying bunkers, administer to the wounded pride of the unsuccessful, and turn legislator at a crowded teeing-ground; he must even at times serve as a foil to the wrath of the disconsolate player who has 'foozled' a drive that was confidently expected to carry him safely beyond a formidable hazard. There are caddies and caddies, to be sure, but when of the right sort, no servants, I fancy, receive such marked evidence of their master's regard. Most of them are Scotch, and some of them the most picturesque figures on the golfing-green.

To obtain a full appreciation of the charms and difficulties of golf you should have acquired a settled conviction of its inferiority as a game requiring either skill or experience; you must have looked upon it with supreme contempt, and catalogued it as a sport for invalids and old men. When you have reached this frame of mind go out on to the links and try it. I never believed a club could be held in so many different ways but the right one until I essayed golf, nor dreamed it so difficult to drive a ball in a given direction. The devotion of the golfer to his game is only equalled by the contempt of him who looks upon it for the first time. You wonder at a great many things when you first see it played, but your wonderment is greatest that a game which appears so simple should have created such a furor.

The secret of its fascination rests largely in the fact that it beats the player, and he, in his perversity, strives the harder to secure the unattainable.

The game is by no means easy; in fact, one of England's foremost players asserts that it takes six months of steady play to acquire consistent form. You must hit the ball properly to send it in the desired direction, and you must deal with it as you find it; you cannot arrange the ball to suit your better advantage, nor await a more satisfactory one, as in baseball and cricket. The club must be held correctly and swung accurately in order to properly address the ball, from which the player should never take his eye, while at the same time he must move absolutely freely, and yet maintain an exact balance. Besides which, it demands judgment and good temper, and if you fail in the latter your play will be weakened on the many trying occasions that arise.

It is a selfish game, where each man fights for himself, seizing every technicality for his own advantage, and there is no doubt that to this fact its popularity may in a large measure be attributed. Unlike cricket, baseball, or football, one is not dependent on others for play. You can usually find some one to make up a match, or

'The duties of the caddie are manifold ... and some of them are the most picturesque figures on the golfing green.' Martin Gwilt Jolley's painting proves the point.

you may go over the course alone, getting the best of practice and fairly good sport, or at least there is always a caddie to be had for the asking, and the usual small fee.

The exercise may be gentle, but whosoever fancies golf does not test the nerves should play a round on popular links.

I cannot say if the native views it in the same light, but I concluded before I had half finished my tour that the attraction of golf was as much due to the atmosphere of tradition on the links and good-fellowship in the clubs as to the qualities of the game itself. I doubt if we in America will ever be able to extract so much pleasure from it. Our dispositions, our temperaments, are not golf-like; we hurry through life at too rapid a gait; we have not the time to give golf in order to gain that responsive charm the game holds for the leisurely suitor.

C. W. Whitney, *Harpers Monthly Magazine*, 1894

MORTIMER STURGIS

From this point onward Mortimer Sturgis proved the truth of what I said to you about the perils of taking up golf at an advanced age. A lifetime of observing my fellow-creatures has convinced me that Nature intended us all to be golfers. In every human being the germ of golf is implanted at birth, and suppression causes it to grow and grow till – it may be at forty, fifty, sixty – it suddenly bursts its bonds and sweeps over the victim like a tidal wave. The wise man, who begins to play in childhood, is enabled to let the poison exude gradually from his system, with no harmful results. But a man like Mortimer Sturgis, with thirty-eight golfless years behind him, is swept off his feet. He is carried away. He loses all sense of proportion. He is like the fly that happens to be sitting on the wall of the dam just when the crack comes.

Mortimer Sturgis gave himself up without a struggle to an orgy of golf such as I have never witnessed in any man. Within two days of that first lesson he had accumulated a collection of clubs large enough to have enabled him to open a shop; and he went on buying them at the rate of two and three a day. On Sundays, when it was impossible to buy clubs, he was like a lost spirit. True, he would do his regular four rounds on the day of rest, but he never felt happy. The thought, as he sliced into the rough, that the patent wooden-faced cleek which he intended to purchase next morning might have made all the difference, completely spoiled his enjoyment.

I remember him calling me up on the telephone at three o'clock one morning to tell me that he had solved the problem of putting. He intended in future, he said, to use a croquet mallet, and he wondered that no one had ever thought of it before. The sound of his broken groan when I informed him that croquet mallets were against the rules haunted me for days.

His golf library kept pace with his collection of clubs. He bought all the

'The perils of taking up golf at an advanced age.' Veteran film star Victor Mature navigating his way around Moor Park during the 1986 Four Stars Pro-Am tournament.

standard works, subscribed to all the golfing papers, and, when he came across a paragraph in a magazine to the effect that Mr Hutchings, an ex-amateur champion, did not begin to play till he was past forty, and that his opponent in the final, Mr S. H. Fry, had never held a club till his thirty-fifth year, he had it engraved on vellum and framed and hung up beside his shaving-mirror.

And Betty, meanwhile? She, poor child, stared down the years into a bleak future, in which she saw herself parted for ever from the man she loved, and the golf-widow of another for whom – even when he won a medal for lowest net at a weekly handicap with a score of a hundred and three minus twenty-four – she could feel nothing warmer than respect. Those were dreary days for Betty. We three – she and I and Eddie Denton – often talked over Mortimer's strange obsession. Denton said that, except that Mortimer had not come out in pink spots, his symptoms were almost identical with those of the dreaded *mongo-mongo*, the scourge of the West African hinterland. Poor Denton! He had already booked his passage for Africa, and spent hours looking in the atlas for good deserts.

In every fever of human affairs there comes at last the crisis. We may emerge from it healed or we may plunge into still deeper depths of soul-sickness; but always the crisis comes. I was privileged to be present when it came in the affairs of Mortimer Sturgis and Betty Weston.

I had gone into the club-house one afternoon at an hour when it is usually empty, and the first thing I saw, as I entered the main room, which looks out on the ninth green, was Mortimer. He was grovelling on the floor, and I confess that, when I caught sight of him, my heart stood still. I feared that his reason, sapped by dissipation, had given way. I knew that for weeks, day in and day out, the niblick had hardly ever been out of his hand, and no constitution can stand that.

Never known for his ability on the greens, Arnold Palmer shows off some of his collection of putters.

He looked up as he heard my footstep.

'Hallo,' he said. 'Can you see a ball anywhere?'

'A ball?' I backed away, reaching for the door-handle. 'My dear boy,' I said soothingly, 'you have made a mistake. Quite a natural mistake. One anybody would have made. But, as a matter of fact, this is the club-house. The links are outside there. Why not come away with me very quietly and let us see if we can't find some balls on the links? If you will wait here a moment, I will call up Doctor Smithson. He was telling me only this morning that he wanted a good spell of ball-hunting to put him in shape. You don't mind if he joins us?'

'It was a Silver King with my initials on it,' Mortimer went on, not heeding me. 'I got on the ninth green in eleven with a nice mashie-niblick, but my approach-putt was a little too strong. It came in through that window.'

I perceived for the first time that one of the windows facing the course was broken, and my relief was great. I went down on my knees and helped him in his search. We ran the ball to earth finally inside the piano.

'What's the local rule?' inquired Mortimer. 'Must I play it where it lies, or may I tee up and lose a stroke? If I have to play it where it lies, I suppose a niblick would be the club?'

It was at this moment that Betty came in. One glance at her pale, set face told me that there was to be a scene, and I would have retired, but that she was between me and the door.

'Hallo, dear,' said Mortimer, greeting her with a friendly waggle of his niblick. 'I'm bunkered in the piano. My approach-putt was a little strong, and I over-ran the green.'

'Mortimer,' said the girl, tensely, 'I want to ask you one question.'

'Yes, dear? I wish, darling, you could have seen my drive at the eighth just now. It was a pip!'

Betty looked at him steadily.

'Are we engaged,' she said, 'or are we not?'

'Engaged? Oh, to be married? Why, of course. I tried the open stance for a change, and...'

'This morning you promised to take me for a ride. You never appeared. Where were you?'

'Just playing golf.'

'Golf! I'm sick of the very name!'

A spasm shook Mortimer.

'You mustn't let people hear you saying things like that!' he said. 'I somehow felt, the moment I began my up-swing, that everything was going to be all right. I...'

'I'll give you one more chance. Will you take me for a drive in your car this evening?'

'I can't.'

'Why not? What are you doing?'

'Just playing golf!'

'I'm tired of being neglected like this!' cried Betty, stamping her foot. Poor girl, I saw her point of view. It was bad enough for her being engaged to the wrong man, without having him treat her as a mere acquaintance. Her conscience fighting with her love for Eddie Denton had kept her true to Mortimer, and Mortimer accepted the sacrifice with an absent-minded carelessness which would have been galling to any girl. 'We might just as well not be engaged at all. You never take me anywhere.'

'I asked you to come with me to watch the Open Championship.'

'Why don't you ever take me to dances?'

'I can't dance.'

'You could learn.'

'But I'm not sure if dancing is a good thing for a fellow's game. You never hear of any first-class pro dancing. James Braid doesn't dance.'

'Well, my mind's made up. Mortimer, you must choose between golf and me.'

'But, darling, I went round in a hundred and one yesterday. You can't expect a fellow to give up golf when he's at the top of his game.'

'Very well. I have nothing more to say. Our engagement is at an end.'

'Don't throw me over, Betty,' pleaded Mortimer, and there was that in his voice which cut me to the heart. 'You'll make me so miserable. And, when I'm miserable, I always slice my approach shots.'

Betty Weston drew herself up. Her face was hard.

'Here is your ring!' she said, and swept from the room.

For a moment after she had gone Mortimer remained very still, looking at the glistening circle in his hand. I stole across the room and patted his shoulder.

'Bear up, my boy, bear up!' I said.

He looked at me piteously.

'Stymied!' he muttered.

'Be brave!'

He went on, speaking as if to himself.

'I had pictured – ah, how often I had pictured! – our little home! Hers and mine. She sewing in her arm-chair, I practising putts on the hearth-rug...' He choked. 'While in the corner, little Harry Vardon Sturgis played with little J. H. Taylor Sturgis. And round the room – reading, busy with their childish tasks – little George Duncan Sturgis, Abe Mitchell Sturgis, Harold Hilton Sturgis, Edward Ray Sturgis, Horace Hutchinson Sturgis, and little James Braid Sturgis.'

'My boy! My boy!' I cried.

'What's the matter?'

'Weren't you giving yourself rather a large family?'

He shook his head moodily.

'Was I?' he said, dully. 'I don't know. What's bogey?'

There was a silence.

'And yet...' he said, at last, in a low voice. He paused. An odd, bright look had come into his eyes. He seemed suddenly to be himself again, the old happy Mortimer Sturgis I had known so well. 'And yet,' he said, 'who knows? Perhaps it is all for the best. They might all have turned out tennis-players!' He raised his niblick again, his face aglow. 'Playing thirteen!' he said. 'I think the game here would be to chip out through the door and work round the club-house to the green, don't you?'

Little remains to be told. Betty and Eddie have been happily married for years. Mortimer's handicap is now down to eighteen, and he is improving all the time. He was not present at the wedding, being unavoidably detained by a medal tournament; but, if you turn up the files and look at the list of presents, which were both numerous and costly, you will see – somewhere in the middle of the column, the words:

STURGIS, J. MORTIMER.

Two dozen Silver King Golf-balls and one patent Sturgis Aluminium Self-Adjusting, Self-Compensating Putting-Cleek.

P. G. Wodehouse, *A Mixed Threesome*

OXFORD GOLF

Unless Mr Darwin is able to adduce convincing evidence to the contrary, I shall continue to believe that the Great Golf Boom made more difference to social life in Oxford than anywhere else in England. Certainly Cambridge is the only place which can dispute the distinction. According to custom, we of Oxford shall not allow her claim to superiority in this or any other matter to succeed without a struggle. The great service which golf has rendered, in possibly varying degrees, to both Universities is the fusion of classes whose individual members occasionally, and on places other than the links, find themselves in antagonism. Tutors and pupils are prone to regard lectures, statutes, and the like from opposite points of view, and are led thereby to underrate the good qualities each of the other. But when they golf with one another the bunkered don reveals his humanity to the undergraduate, and on his side learns that his junior is not so lacking as might have been supposed in the virtues of discretion and persistency.

Of late years golf has been responsible for a remarkable development in both classes of three notable virtues – early rising, punctuality, and abstinence: it has also taught seniors the value of terseness in literary expression. So many members of the University Golf Club are furiously anxious to strike off the first teeing grounds at Radley and Cowley somewhere between 1.15 and 2.30 during the winter months, that nine o'clock has come to be regarded as quite a reasonable time for a business interview between teacher and taught. In consequence, the disciplinary officers of the various colleges seldom find it necessary to admonish the golfers among their undergraduate members for insufficient attendance at morning chapel or roll-call. And these men go to those functions in their coats and hosen, if not in their hats. They do not slip an overcoat over pyjamas specially purchased for their resemblance to grey flannel trousers, nor do they return to bed after satisfying the requirements of the Dean. There is a provident purposefulness about their rising. Only Professors and 'bloods', the excrescences, so to speak, on Oxford society, can begin to golf 'not only after teeing the ball but also immediately after breakfasting themselves', as Mr Godley's translation of Aristotle's unpublished works hath it. The normal man, be he don or undergraduate, must get his morning's work done before he can, with mind free and conscience clear, tackle the important event of the day. Therefore lecturers frequently expound, and undergraduates sometimes attend, at nine o'clock of the morning, a full hour earlier than was customary twenty years ago. Later in the day, as the moment approaches when he who wishes to complete his round in daylight must get him on his bicycle and race similarly intentioned men uphill to Radley or downhill to Cowley, the estimate set on the value of punctuality increases wonderfully. The golfing don reserves his sharpest sarcasms for men who are late at the noon lecture, and his remarks are invariably applauded by a large section of his audience. That applause is nothing to the approbation which meets his recommendation to 'look that point up for yourselves later', commonly uttered as the hour-hand of the clock approaches the figure I. By the time it has touched it the orator and many of his audience have changed their clothes and eaten their luncheon. Lay opinion holds that golfers as a class favour apolausticism rather than abstinence. At Oxford circumstances make it necessary for the regular players to practise at luncheon time a frugality which is good at once for their pockets and their health.

Outsiders share to some extent in the amenities which golf has brought into the life of the University. In days not very long past an invitation to dine at the high table in a college hall was not to be accepted without qualms of apprehension by one whose scholarship had rusted. Possibly his fear that the conversation would be above his head was not always well grounded, but there is no doubt that he had to face risks. Nowadays he may feel tolerably certain that at least at the beginning and towards the end of the evening the subject of golf will be mentioned. It is quite likely that he will gain confidence by observing that his neighbour displays one of the two marks which most readily denote the golf-player: they are a callus at the base of the left forefinger and an incipient bruise under the left eye. He will be quite safe if, noting the presence of one or the other sign, he opens a discussion on the merits of the overlapping grip, or the best means to avoid taking the ball heavy.

A. C. M. Croome, *The Royal & Ancient Game of Golf*, 1912

PLAYING FOR A SIMPSON

A *ball* on the match is a good thing. It is a tangible result of victory, a punishment to the loser, a reward to the winner. It is such a small affair that the keenest nosed moralist can scarcely detect in it the smell of gambling, but small as it is it secures careful play and teaches the player to overcome nervousness, for in a good match its loss or its gain generally depends on the last putt. Sir Walter Simpson strongly advocates *half-a-crown* as the ordinary stake, and a good many, out of respect for him, and for the coin, have adopted his recommendation. This has added a new word to the golfing vocabulary. Two North Berwick players of Simpsonian views who have always been averse (and rightly so), from letting their caddies into the pecuniary secrets of the match, have for some time gone on playing for a *Simpson*, but through the frequent use of the word, and the passage of the article to and fro at the close of the matches their secret seems to have got out, for we now hear of more than one couple who play for a *Simpson*, and thus contribute toward the immortality of Sir Walter!

Letter to *Golfer* Magazine from A Concerned Reader, December 1890

GOLFLUENZA

Golf is not a mere game; it is a disease, infectious and contagious, which once acquired cannot be shaken off. Once a golfer always a golfer – there's no help for it!

The game exercises a spell, a thrall over the man who has once swung a club. You begin promiscuously and experimentally. A golfing friend casually hands you a driving iron and asks you to have a 'whang' at a golf ball. Well! You 'whang' and your fate is sealed. You are a golfer from that moment. Most likely you missed the ball and, like the man who ordered another pound of beetle powder, vowing that 'he'd kill that confounded cockroach before he'd done', you mutter between your teeth that you'll go on whanging till you knock that ball into the next field. Or you, by the veriest chance (as you discover later), give the ball a fine swinging smack and to your delight see the lively bit of white gutta-percha soaring in the air to alight a full hundred yards off.

Then with a mild chuckle you hand back your friend his iron and exultantly observe that you think this game would 'suit you' thoroughly. Whatever your luck – whether you hit or whether you miss – you are a golf-infected person. The incipient stages of the disease are rapid. You buy a set of clubs, clandestinely and ill-advisedly, seeking no advice, and probably acquiring tools which indeed prove 'ill adapted for putting the little balls into the little holes'. Then you sally forth covertly to practice and to fret away your soul in vain endeavours to 'drive'. You

'Once a golfer always a golfer – there's no help for it!' These hardy players demonstrate the truth of it in snow-covered Rye in 1982.

practise 'putting' – which looks so easy, but is so tricky – on your lawn, and you fume and perspire at your own ineptitude.

L. Latchford, *The Young Man*, 1903

THE GHOST OF COLONEL BOGEY

There is a 'Colonel Bogey' at every Golf links in the kingdom. Some golfers in their ignorance regard him as a mythical personage, who we play against in order that he may play with us – as a cat does with a mouse. Nothing of the kind. He is the spirit of a departed golfer.

Have you ever noticed a golfer whom everyone knows, and yet no one knows? His past history is obscure, but his present and future are painfully patent. He is a golfer who has taken up the game late in life, and has been bitten with the craze in its deadliest form. Some golfers escape his fate because they die, or commit suicide, or are dragged to Bedlam. Better that, than the end waiting for this poor wretch. Sore stricken with the mania, he struggles round the links weekly, daily, hourly. His days are one long foozle, his nights a hideous nightmare.

Then a change comes over the scene. The iron has entered his soul. Heaven save the mark! Better a thousand times that he had remained a guileless, foozling, Christian old gentleman. His game improves by leaps and bounds. Simple golfers are astounded, but the wise grow fearsome. He becomes, if not the best player in the club, the most deadly. The handicapping committee are nonplussed, he carries everything before him. He does not smoke or drink, and he only swears in obscure parts of the course, and in tones deep and guttural and in language strange to human ears. Hanging lies have a fascination for him, and he revels in a stymie.

And so he plays on, regardless of the tender feelings of the handicapping committee, winning gold medals galore, scooping the half-crowns of the ardent novice, and breaking records right and left until – until what? Until the end comes and his spirit leaves the clay, to fly to the newest links – inland by preference, where his ghost becomes the 'Bogey' of the green. Why do we top our drives, foozle our iron shots, miss ridiculous putts? Because his spirit is always with us annulling our best efforts.

Do you see that irascible-looking golfer on the last green? He has got an eighteen-inch putt, to save the match. If he holes the ball his wife and children will have a week of blissful happiness. If he misses – why, heaven help them! His caddie hands him his putter. It is a momentous occasion, and the silence of death falls on the little group. Wise men shake their heads, they recognise that he is fighting with an unseen force. Slowly he squats down and takes his line. Only eighteen inches separate his ball from the hole, and the green is as level as a billiard-table. But he sees a hog's back, four worm casts, and a tricky slope. Back goes the putter and then forward, there is a faint click, the ball speeds forwards towards but (alas! for his wife and children) not into the hole. Both men swear, the loser with savage emphasis, the winner, out of assumed sympathy and softly as if he was pronouncing a benediction. Some men there are who escape the fascination of this demon. These men are dull-witted or imbecile, or men who never drink water, or pray, or go to church, or men possessed of a handy trick of blasphemy.

Long Spoon, *Golf*, 1897

DRIVING TO DESTRUCTION

If a good golfing temperament were not a *sine qua non* to success on the links, there would be many more players of first rank. Golfers there are by the score who are capable of playing the game with accuracy and power, and when things are going well of doing brilliant deeds; and yet they somehow or other fail when we most hope and expect that they will succeed. And this failure may, I fancy, not infrequently be laid at the door of mental rather than physical causes. The flesh is able, the muscles are fit, the eye is keen, the knowledge is sufficient, but the mind cannot control and govern the whole man. It has been said by one well able from experience both of life and golf to give a good judgment, that golf is a game which is always fighting against the player.

That golf is an irritating game anyone who has played it seriously knows, and recognises also that the man who loses his temper as a rule loses also the match. 'I know it's only a damned game,' shouted an eminent legal luminary as he snapped his croquet mallet over his knee and then hurled its head through the drawingroom window, but even games require some mastering or they will get the upper hand.

Seve Ballesteros in trouble during the 1994 Volvo Spanish Masters.

'An unfortunate lie' for Mark Roe. What sort of shot was required to get the ball there is anyone's guess.

Nothing is more annoying than, after a good drive, to find one's self hampered for the next stroke by an unfortunate lie. Among the many ways of improving golf that have been suggested, a proposal that every ball should be 'teed' seemed to me, at the time it was made, to be the most destructive.

J. C. Law, *The Irish Golfer*, 1902

SOME GOLF DISEASES

I Mendacitis Anarithmetica

This is a very strange complaint and is by no means confined to either sex. Ladies, indeed, seem to possess it, even in a more marked degree than men, but then, dear things! They never were good at arithmetic. The chief observable symptom is a total suppression of the sense of strict accuracy, coupled with an absolute inability to make two and two anything more than three. Some wonderful scores have thus been achieved, not of malice prepense, but of sheer want of memory. It is also a peculiarity of such patients that though in reality perfectly conversant with the rules, they are ready to forget them whenever it may be conducive to the making of a good score for them to do so. They will even, in playing through the green, not be too particular as to remove twigs, &c., upon which their ball may be actually lying, and if such removal cause the ball to roll out of its position, even say for six or eight inches, they will not be concerned or even disposed to incur the penalty provided for such illegal performances. If you do not catch them *in flagrante delicto*, nothing is said; if you do, they invariably plead ignorance of the rule, even though you may have on many previous occasions called their attention to and explained it.

Abe Mitchell demonstrating how to escape from a bunker one-handed. A famous professional in the 1920s, and a great friend of Samuel Ryder, he was the model for the tiny figure on top of the Ryder Cup trophy.

In bunkers, as a matter of habit and precaution, they invariably leave the truth outside – indeed, I have seen them after having landed their tee-shot in the bunker specially provided for such players, emerge, almost triumphantly therefrom, after about five or six minutes solid hard work, and heard them say, with a beaming countenance, as if flushed with triumph, '2!' or if in a *very* gracious mood, '3!' when you know really that these figures represent dozens and not units as they would have you believe. Finally, according to their reckoning they may do the hole – a bogey 6 – in 5, and win it, as they think, from you; and when, as if by accident, you examine their ball, point out at least 10 or 12 separate and distinct mementoes of the niblick, and remind them that the ball was a new one at that tee, they frankly avow that they 'cannot make that out, but perhaps it was 6 and *not* 5 after all'.

In competitions they are rather dangerous. They think all the time that you are trying to cheat them, so that you may win yourself, quite regardless of the fact that in order to play a good game, all your energies should be devoted to that end, instead of being constantly required in the well-nigh hopeless task of rectifying their imperfect memory. Sometimes on putting greens, a player of this type has been known quite accidentally to move the ball an inch or more, whereupon without your having said a word, he will turn round and say to you, almost angrily, 'That *wasn't* a stroke, the ball *never* moved.' Should you show him how far it moved from its original position, he will probably say, 'Oh! *That* doesn't count.'

There is only one way to deal with players of this class. Firmly implant on your memory, and on your caddy's, the resting place of the ball after each stroke, and as firmly but courteously, insist on the total number being placed on the card, without allowing *any* discussion after, say, the first three holes or so. You can generally convince the patient about these, and when he sees that you are watching and counting, and that the caddies are doing so as well, he will probably begin to count accurately himself, which greatly simplifies matters.

II Polyclubia Inanis

This is a very peculiar disease, being by no manner of means confined to beginners; in fact, it often reaches an acute form of mania in otherwise very fine players. It consists of an inconquerable desire to be possessed of any certain club with which either the rightful owner in the patient's presence, or the patient himself when trying it, has made a fine shot. He generally endeavours to acquire the club, and I am bound to say is willing to pay a price quite incommensurate with its real value. Consequently clubs accumulate to an almost alarming degree.

Some one club has a finer ring in the metal than another, but doesn't lie right or is too heavy, so he alters the weight (he generally rubs this down at home), then has the lie adapted to his special requirements, then has another shaft put in, because the original shaft was 'no good', then plays with it for one round, keeps the ball pretty straight, in fact, does wonders with it; presently swears by the club, having found at last what he had been looking for so long. Later on in the day he happens

to pull a ball with the self-same club, vows he never held a more rotten contrivance in his hands and either straightway gives it away or sells it for two shillings.

A week, only a week, later, he sees a club in some one else's bag, watches the new owner play with it and make good shots consistently; asks him where he got it (since, of course, with such a multiplicity of clubs individualisation is well-nigh an impossibility), and when told that it is one of his 'cast-offs' he at once borrows it, to get it copied. The copy is never the same as the original, and so the copy soon goes adrift in the same way. Such patients should not be cured too quickly; if they have money galore they *are* incurable; if they have not, the disease works out its own salvation. If the victim contented himself with, and limited his practice to, only five or six well-selected clubs, he would probably play a better game; but he still firmly and ineradicably believes that it is not the fine player but the fine club that makes the fine shot.

Timothy Ward, *Golfing Magazine*, 1899

Spreading the gospel of golf. Professional W.G. Oke handing out golf clubs at a holiday camp in Minehead in 1938.

'A wise old caddie'
keeps his thoughts to
himself.

TEMPERAMENT IN GOLF

When one has the misfortune to play against 'the man with a temper', the very greatest tact and knowledge of human nature are necessary, if one is to attempt to soothe his savage breast. 'Touch not the cat without the glove.' But the devastating and demoralising effect of the golfing temper, on even the finest natures, is so terrible, that it is extremely dangerous to say anything, however apparently sympathetic, and the patient is much better left severely alone, until the paroxysm has passed. The breaking of the club wherewith the fatal stroke has been delivered, is a common symptom in such cases; and usually, this sacrifice is less an act of reprisal on the club itself, than a solemn protest and testimony against the injustice of which the golfer conceives himself to be the victim, and a necessary step towards the rehabilitation of his mind. The angry golfer has been known to relieve his pent-up feelings by hurling his club far from him, after the failure of his stroke. This is an extremely dangerous habit, as, in his anger, the golfer is frequently careless of the direction in which his club flies, and his partner will do well to keep an eye on his movements. Like the 'fatalist', 'the man with a temper' had better be avoided, whenever possible. No pleasurable game is to be had in such company, and their habits are extremely infectious.

If players would only treat others as they would wish others to treat themselves, the harmony and pleasure of the game would be greatly enhanced. The well-balanced mind will not be unhinged by the untoward chances of golf. The wise golfer recognises, that but for these alterations of luck, the game would cease to amuse or charm, and if he has more than his share of bad luck, or bad play, to-day, he says nothing about it, being sure that to-morrow, things will go better for him. To go on inventing reasons for one's bad play is fatal to improvement, and can only annoy and irritate one's partner. 'Deeds, not words,' is the true golfer's motto.

'In my opinion,' said a wise old caddie, 'a man sud niver mak' excuses for hisself at gowf. It's like bein' disrespectfu' to Providence. Gowfers sud jist tak' things as they come and be contentit. In my opeenion some fowks like to shaw off a bit by bletherin' aboot their bad play.'

Garden G. Smith, *The World of Golf*, (The Isthmian Library), 1898

THAT'S MY EXCUSE

The average golfer is prolific in excuses. No doubt, as the number of his bad strokes decreases, he will indulge in fewer explanatory remarks. From the persistent way in which players proffer excuses, we must infer that this 'escape of steam' has an ameliorative effect upon their tempers.

I have seen a golfer of a choleric temperament striving manfully to keep calm. It was a not uninteresting spectacle. All went well for a few holes, until, after a succession of poor shots, he would give way to a horrid imprecation, and then fling his club after the ball. Other men, in similar circumstances, occasionally hit the ground savagely with their clubs until they break them. Such manifestations of the natural man are regrettable, but they are rather uncommon.

While the number of excuses is legion, perhaps the most popular is a sudden attack of indigestion. A winning player has rarely anything to complain of. Not so the man who is holes behind, and likely to remain so until the match is over. If he happens to be playing very badly, he will speedily remark, 'I'm out of form to-day. I've been suffering from indigestion for several days.' His opponent smiles inwardly, if that is a possible feat; but vocally he is quite sympathetic. 'Indigestion is a most troublesome thing,' he will admit, and then he may go on to describe one of his own recent attacks.

The married man – more especially the young married man – has an excellent reason for his bad play. His excuse has done duty to a thousand times, and it is not in the least likely to be dethroned from its position of favouritism. The baby is often restless at nights, and the loving husband, anxious to conserve his darling wife's strength, willingly attends to 'the bottles'. This labour of love interrupts the husband's slumbers, and, if it should occur on a Friday night, its effects are seen next day in the erratic strokes from the tee and the faulty pitches to the green. 'I had a disturbed night,' is a good phrase, and one that is thoroughly understood by every Benedick.

Dogs frequently afford legitimate excuses for a poor stroke. A terrier will

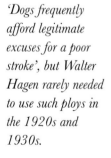

'Dogs frequently afford legitimate excuses for a poor stroke', but Walter Hagen rarely needed to use such ploys in the 1920s and 1930s.

sometimes dash in front of a player who is about to strike the ball, and, if a foozle is made in the circumstances, the golfer's complaint is obviously well-grounded. The 'meh' of a sheep has often an unsteadying influence. I have seen a player interrupted three times by a sheep, which coolly and, as it seemed, deliberately raised its voice in protest, just at the very moment that the club was about to be drawn away from the ball.

Most of us make bad strokes at golf – some more, some less – but the impaired digestion, the bad night's rest, and the yaup of the mongrel have not so much to do with the unsatisfactory results as some players imagine.

If the lie of the ball were studied more, and the distance to the hole carefully measured by the eye, I am convinced there would be fewer weak approaches.

What is called playing 'wi' the heid' is simply using one's eyes and judgment to the best advantage. The thoughtful, observant player will make greater progress at the game than the man who plays it in a happy-go-lucky manner

Bulger, *Echoes From the Links*, 1924

ON NERVE AND TRAINING

Of all the games in which the soul of the Anglo-Saxon delights, there is perhaps none which is a severer test of that mysterious quality called 'nerve' than the game of golf. It is a game in which a very great deal is apt to depend upon a single stroke – indeed, upon each single stroke throughout the round – and it is at the same time a game which calls for delicately-measured strokes, and, consequently, for steadiness and control of hand.

'I cannot understand it at all,' a famous tiger-slayer was once heard to exclaim, in desperation. 'I have shot tigers in India, knowing that my life depended upon the steadiness of my aim, and could swear that the ball would go true through the heart; but here is a wretched little putt, a foot and a half long, and I miss it of very nervousness!'

Singularly enough, it is just these short little putts – those which there is no excuse for missing, and which, in practice, we should infallibly hole, almost without taking aim – that are the great trials of nerve in the big match. The somewhat longer putts are far less trying, and it is just because there is no excuse for missing that our too active imaginations picture to us how foolish we shall look if we fail, and thus suggest to us a sufficient cause for failure. It is very silly, but it is very human.

Is there any means, then, to be found by which we may cultivate confidence, and silence our morbid imaginings? In a great degree, confidence depends upon health, and upon the spontaneous, harmonious action of eye and hand. We all know how, on those black days when eye and hand are not working well together,

Golf 'is a game in which a very great deal' can depend on a single stroke, as Bernhard Langer found out when this missed putt in the 1991 Ryder Cup gave victory to the Americans.

purely imaginary difficulties are apt to present themselves upon the smoothest surface of the simplest putt. How rubs and depressions, which are invisible to every eye except our own, appear as insurmountable obstacles, though they have no existence outside of our fancy. Nevertheless, if we fancy our molehill a mountain, we shall need all sorts of scaling ladders and alpenstocks.

There have been golfers who have doctored themselves with such soothing drugs as opium and laudanum to lull their nervous excitability; and no doubt, without recourse to such heroic remedies as these, we may do much for ourselves, according to our individual temperaments, by a clear understanding and discrimination of the uses and abuses of tobacco. But the great point is that we should not try to train ourselves 'too fine' – we should not be too healthful. When our liver is energetic, and our pulses are bounding through our veins: when we feel, in fact, that the Sphinx of Golf has yielded up her every secret, and we go forth over-confident to the 'tee' – then is the very time that it will be revealed to us that we are in a fool's paradise – that it is not this abnormal flow of healthfulness that will bring us success in the game; but that it is our ordinary rather muddle-headed condition that is the most conducive to that stupid, dogged, persistence of hard work which only earns its well-deserved reward.

Horace Hutchinson, *Golf*, Badminton Library, 1890

ANATOMIST'S TRIBUTE TO GOLF

Golf is a game which, like all others, has its fluctuations, but, unlike, others, it stays. *The par-4, tenth hole*
The reason for this is not difficult to find. It is contained in an article written by the *at the Belfry, scene of*
Senior Demonstrator in Anatomy at the University of Glasgow: 'Golf is the *many dramatic Ryder*
perfection of an outdoor game. It implies walking at a steady pace without hurry *Cup clashes in recent*
or excitement, abundant, though not excessive, exercise to the arms, an education *years.*
to the eye in estimating distances, and a training in graduating the amount of force
to be used to send the ball the needful distance, and the niceties of the game afford
an educational influence of great variety and high order.'

Leamington Spa Advertiser, 1897

WARDING OFF THE BRAIN STORM

Not long ago two golfers, close friends, were playing over a California course. A
dispute over scores led to the fatal shooting of one and the committing suicide by
the other. Physicians agreed that the man who did the shooting temporarily was
insane. Yet, just how much of a gap existed between the mental status of the golfer
who did the shooting and the wrathful fury many otherwise sane golfers allow to
lay hold of themselves?

The guns here were carried not to settle arguments over the score, but in case of German parachutists landing during the early years of the war.

How many 'dubs' have you seen in sand traps with hunted looks on their faces, slashing madly and wildly at balls which figuratively they could not see because of blind rage?

Warding off the 'brain storm' which is wont to follow in the path of an inglorious trouncing in competition is not the easiest thing to do, but five minutes concentration devoted to the subject of the physical drain such a malady has upon man or woman sometimes will serve as a cure. 'Nothing could have been lost, as nothing had been gained in that match.' Is not that reasoning sound enough?

Why pay dues at a club for the privilege of working yourself into a fury? Get your money's worth!

Frank C. Tone, *The American*, 1928

A GAME FOR ALL

It is a game for the many. It suits all sorts and conditions of men. The strong and the weak, the halt and the maimed, the octogenarian and the boy, the rich and the poor, the clergyman and the infidel, may play every day, except Sunday. The late riser can play comfortably, and be back for his rubber in the afternoon; the sanguine man can measure himself against those who will beat him; the half-crown

Golf 'is a game for the many. It suits all sorts and conditions of men.' John Daly, 1995 British Open champion.

seeker can find victims, the gambler can bet, the man of high principle, by playing for nothing, may enjoy himself, and yet feel good. You can brag, and lose matches; depreciate yourself, and win them. Unlike the other Scotch game of whisky-drinking, excess in it is not injurious to the health.

Golf has some drawbacks. It is possible, by too much of it, to destroy the mind... For the golfer, Nature loses her significance. Larks, the casts of worms, the buzzing of bees, and even children are hateful to him. I have seen a golfer very angry at getting into a bunker by killing a bird, and rewards of as much as ten shillings have been offered for boys maimed on the links. Rain comes to be regarded solely in its relation to the putting greens; the daisy is detested, botanical specimens are but 'hazards', twigs 'break clubs'. Winds cease to be east, south, west, or north. They are ahead, behind, or sideways, and the sky is bright or dark, according to the state of the game.

Sir Walter Simpson, *The Art of Golf*, 1887

SOME OF THE HUMOURS OF GOLF

A tolerable day, a tolerable green, a tolerable opponent, supply, or ought to supply, all that any reasonably constituted human being should require in the way of entertainment. With a fine sea view, and a clear course in front of him, the golfer should find no difficulty in dismissing all worries from his mind, and regarding golf,

'A tolerable day, a tolerable green.' Possibly the most scenic sight in golf, the Masters at Augusta.

even it may be indifferent golf, as the true and adequate end of man's existence. Care may sit behind the horseman, she never presumes to walk with the caddie. No inconvenient reminiscences of the ordinary workaday world, no intervals of weariness or monotony interrupt the pleasures of the game. And of what other recreation can this be said? Does a man trust to conversation to occupy his leisure moments? He is at the mercy of fools and bores. Does he put his trust in shooting, hunting, or cricket? Even if he be so fortunately circumstanced as to obtain them in perfection, it will hardly be denied that such moments of pleasure as they can afford are separated by not infrequent intervals of tedium. The ten-mile walk through the rain after missing a stag; a long ride home after a blank day; fielding out while your opponents score 400, cannot be described by the most enthusiastic deer-stalker, fox-hunter, or cricketer, as otherwise than wearisome episodes in delightful pursuits. Lawn tennis, again, is not so much a game as an exercise, while in real tennis or in rackets something approaching to equality of skill between the players would seem to be almost necessary for enjoyment. These more violent exercises, again, cannot be played with profit for more than one or two hours in the day. And while this may be too long for a man very hard worked in other ways, it is too short for a man who wishes to spend a complete holiday as much as possible in the open air.

Moreover, all these games have the demerit of being adapted principally to the season of youth. Long before middle life is reached, rowing, rackets, fielding at cricket, are a weariness to those who once excelled at them. At thirty-five, when strength and endurance may be at their maximum, the particular elasticity required for these exercises is seriously diminished. The man who has gloried in them as the most precious of his requirements begins, so far as they are concerned, to grow old; and growing old is not commonly supposed to be so agreeable an operation in itself as to make it advisable to indulge in it more often in a single lifetime than is absolutely necessary. The golfer, on the other hand, is never old until he is decrepit. So long as Providence allows him the use of two legs active enough to carry him round the green, and of two arms supple enough to take a 'half swing', there is no reason why his enjoyment in the game need be seriously diminished. Decay no doubt there is; long driving has gone for ever; and something less of firmness and accuracy may be noted even in the short game. But the decay has come by such slow gradations, it has delayed so long and spared so much, that it is robbed of half its bitterness.

A. J. Balfour, *Golf*, Badminton Library, 1890

THE CHARMS OF GOLF

A gentleman at St Andrews once made a match to play level with a brother golfer who was a far stronger player than himself, on the understanding only that he should be allowed to say 'Booh!' as his opponent was about to strike the ball thrice during

The ultimate gamesmanship? A fly-past by the Red Arrows over the Old Course at St Andrews.

the match. History goes on to relate how, making the most of this concession, he continually stole up behind his opponent (open-mouthed, menacing him, as it were, with a 'booh!') with such disconcerting effect, that the receiver of the three 'boohs!' won the match actually without having used any of his 'boohs!' at all.

Horace Hutchinson, *Golf*, Badminton Library, 1890

GOLF BY A NON-GOLFER

[The Editor received the following communication a few weeks ago from an old friend resident at Eastbourne, and, thinking it might not be out of place to hear the other side of the question, he now gives it publicity. This he does the more readily, because, although much that it contains is both ludicrous and absurd, he knows that the lamentations of the writer are echoed by many excellent old fogies throughout the length and breadth of the land.]

I am writing to you, because I believe you know something about a game called Golf. Some people here object to its being called a game, and prefer to designate it a science. I should term it a disease, or even an epidemic. Its origin I cannot exactly trace, but will just tell you, if you will bear with me, my own experiences of it.

We have, or rather had, one of the nicest little social clubs here you would wish to find; nice rubber of whist, and nice quietly-dressed young fellows playing a quiet game of billiards. It was the very place in all the world for a man whose struggling days were over to sleep himself to his rest with satisfaction. There were beautiful walks. There is a fine common, called the Links, and a lovely cluster of trees appropriately named Paradise. It was my favourite walk. One day, as I strolled over the Links, I saw a party of men in the bottom of a chalk pit engaged, as I surmised, in digging for fossils. I am, as you know, something of a geologist myself. I therefore walked round the chalk pit in order to see if their search was likely to be productive, but by the time I had got round to where it was possible to get down into the pit the men were gone.

The next development was the appearance, in the hall of our little club, of a very large notice board hanging against the wall. It was covered with crimson baize, while above, in gold letters, were the words, 'Royal Eastbourne Golf Club'. I naturally traced no connection between this mystical writing on the wall and my supposed scientists in the chalk pit; but that very evening over our rubber two of our party began to talk in strange tongues. It is very irritating when people talk in a language you cannot understand, and just as bad if they talk in English over a rubber. Any how, as I soon discovered, what they did talk about was Golf, and those diggers at the bottom of the chalk pit were not geologists, but golfers. Bear in mind we play half-crown points, and it is wonderful how expensive a little golf talk comes over a rubber at half-crown points.

Twenties trick-shot specialist Alex J. Morrison proves that nowhere is safe from being hit by a golf ball. Learning from Harry Houdini, he attracted large audiences by demonstrating his skills outside the theatre he was playing.

However, I think I bore up pretty well, because I fancied it would not occur again. Nor was I really seriously harassed when I was one day struck smartly on the kneecap by an exceedingly hard little ball as I was taking my favourite walk. I found out that it was a golf ball, and the owner, hurrying up, told me, with all the air of offering consolation, that he had called 'Four' three times – ('Fore!' the old gentleman means, of course). I replied that it would have been simpler to have called 'Twelve' at once; and he left me promptly, as if I were dangerous.

As I say, however, I did not greatly mind that, because of course I might find another walk for myself. But it got worse and worse. It was quite the exception to hear any conversation in the club that I was able to follow. One by one they were carried off. I began to fancy after a time that as I went into the room I could tell, by a glance at the faces, which had fallen a new victim; for the contagion spread daily. Not only upon the faces of the sufferers were the marks of the dire fever visible, but even in their very habiliments. Respectable gentlemen, who would never in their days of health and sanity have appeared in our fashionable watering place in other garb than that of the walking gentleman of the stage – the morning coat and the hard billycock – now showed themselves in our streets in the most shooting of shooting coats, in knickerbockers, and in the style of head gear known as 'fore and aft.' I have even known a gentleman come into our club and play a rubber in stockings, spats, and knickerbockers!

I was getting rather desperate. Old General H– asked me one day, 'Now what do they say in the club about the probable designs of Russia?'

'They talk of nothing in the club,' I was shamefacedly obliged to answer, 'except Golf!'

I determined that in very self-defence I would try to learn something about this wonderful game, but not by personal experience. No, no, I had seen too much of the dire effects of it on others. But I had heard that you could generally learn more about a subject from one who was commencing its study than from a past master. So I asked my little niece, whom my brother used often to make carry his sticks – clubs is the technical word for them – to write me an essay on the game. This is what she wrote, and I think it is very good: 'The game of golf is a very nice game. Most people like it very much; even babies play when they are quite young.' (This is not to say that they will not play when they are quite old.) 'The balls you play with are very hard indeed, and they might kill anybody if they got hit very hard with them.' (It seems I have been in some danger.) 'When you play golf you first take a little sand and make a little heap, and then place the ball at the top of it; then you take a club called a driver, and hit the ball; that is called driving. Then if you get a good way from the hole, but too close to take a driver, you would take an iron club and play up to the hole; when you are close to the hole you would take a club called a putter; and when you get into the hole you count your strokes, and whoever gets into the hole in the least number of strokes, it is their hole' (this is still technical, and does not mean that you acquire freehold right in the portion of ground occupied by the hole); 'and if two people who are playing get into the hole in the same number of strokes, it is called a halved hole.'

So there! I flatter myself I know something about it now; and when I see any of these gentlemen going about with those great quivers full of sticks over their back, as they do – something like Cupids – I shall be able to tell them what they are all for, and talk away with the best of them. I assure you it is the only way in self-defence. Now they are fond of coming up to me and telling me all about their matches. This bores me, but it would bore me more perhaps if I did not understand about it, for they would tell me just the same. Sometimes they play two aside, and then they make a confidant of me, and talk about their partners. Colonel McBunker came up and told me he had been playing with Major FitzNiblick as his partner, and 'Of course, my dear fellow, of course we lost the match. FitzNiblick *will* stick to that miserable game of running the ball up with the putter. I appeal to you now if it is not too ridiculous?'

I of course replied, as in duty bound, that it was most reprehensible on the part of the FitzNiblick; and the colonel passed on to tell the next man in the club all about it. After a certain succession of golfers, who all appeared to have had the most phenomenally hard luck, I found myself the victim of FitzNiblick himself. 'I can't conceive, my dear fellow,' he said to me, 'how any man in his sober senses could expect to win a match with McBunker. He *will* be always trying to loft the ball up to the hole with his iron – far safer with the putter, I tell him – far safer with the putter.'

I always think there is nothing like candour – and I was anxious to put a stop to these eternal confidences – so I told the FitzNiblick what Colonel McBunker had said to me about his misdeeds with the putter, and then went into the billiard-room to tell the colonel what FitzNiblick had said about his iron play. And then I followed the McBunker back into the card room to see the fun. There was a good deal of fun. They were on the point of seizing each other by the throat, when I took up the tongs and shovel, and by handing the former to the McBunker and the latter to the FitzNiblick, awoke them to a sense of the figure they were cutting before the members of the club. They haven't spoken to each other since, but as they have not spoken to me either I do not mind. They think I am *too* sympathetic, and the golfers are fairly leaving me in peace.

I went out the other day to see a celebrated player who came down from London. I thought, as a resident, I had about as much right on the links as he had, but he ordered me about as if I was in his drawing-room – moved me about like a chessman, by Jove! He was very rude to me once because I made a remark – not to him or even about him – just as he was on the point of playing. And the next time when I was as still as a mouse he found fault with me because 'he thought I was going to move!' However could I help his thoughts? To say nothing of the confounded impertinence of his formulating any idea about my probable actions! At the next hole he picked up a small shell off the ground, and I could not resist taking what perhaps was the liberty (but I felt it to be pardoned by the freemasonry of science) of darting forward and exclaiming to him: 'Ha, my dear sir, I observe you are a conchologist!'

'A what, Sir?' he said, as if he had never heard the word.

'A conchologist, my dear Sir,' said I.

'You're a conchologist yourself, and be hanged to you,' was his polite reply.

Now, perhaps I ought to have felt proud that the finger of science had so set its seal upon my brow, patent to all beholders, but really the tone in which the remark was made seemed to compel me to place some quite different interpretation on what he said. I left that celebrated golfer abruptly. I do not believe that he was a man of science at all, and I am certain he was not a man of courtesy.

I do not think I have much more to say – indeed, you will probably wonder excessively at my object in writing so much; but you understand this wonderful game, science, allegory of human life, epidemic, or whatever you like to call it. It is a wonderful mystery, and very dangerous; it is beyond comprehension. One man told me he could not 'hole a putt', as he called it, while Mr Gladstone was in office, but that no sooner had the Liberal Unionists got into power than he found it plain and simple. Now, what could be the meaning of that?

I had a certain object in writing this to you, all the same. They are getting up golf clubs, not only at Eastbourne, but also at Seaford and Brighton, to my certain knowledge; and doubtless the same danger is threatening many of the like places, where quiet old people retire after the noonday toil of life is over. If you could but give publicity in some way or another to this piteous lamentation it might serve as a warning to others in like station with myself, and enable them to avoid falling into similar – and let me conclude in the golfing vernacular – 'bunkers'.

The Golfing Annual 1887-88, edited by C. Robertson Bauchope

NO PASSING FANCY

We cannot refrain for the life of us from closing our remarks on golfing with some expression of our intense attachment to it. Nor is the attachment a passing fancy, or the offspring of national prejudice. In the alembic of experience many faithful pleasures have been tested and found dross; following back on the trial of our life, we have marked many erring steps; and maturity shakes its head at the wayward fancies of younger days. But thou gentle sprite! whose Empire is the dark green links and whose Votaries wield the bending club and speed the whizzing ball, art as dear to us now in the sere and yellow leaf as when first we flew to share in thy health-inspiring rites with the flush and ardour of boyhood.

H. B. Farnie, *The Golfer's Manual*, 1857

THE ENDLESS VARIETY OF GOLF

Nothing contributes more to the popularity of golf than its almost endless variety. No two courses are the same, even though they be similar in character; no two shots are alike, even though the same distance has to be accomplished. This variety is a very distinct feature of the game. Football or cricket grounds, if good, do not vary much from one another. Certain soils, no doubt, lend themselves better to turf growing

than others, and the sticky patches favour the bowlers, but the conformation of the *Sheik Abdallah,* cricket and football field remains the same. In golf it is quite otherwise; each course *watched by his sons,* has its own features, and each demands a fresh variety of strokes. The play at St *driving off on a course* Andrews or Hoylake is quite different from the play at Sandwich – so different that *near Cairo in 1938.* the clubs suitable for the hard turf of the North Country greens would require modification if used on the softer turf of the South Kent course. The golfer who has grown weary of one set of strokes has only to leave his home green and pay a visit to some other course, and he will find new difficulties to be encountered and have to devise fresh methods of overcoming them. No golfer has ever been forced to say to himself with tears, 'There are no more links to conquer.'

John L. Low, *Concerning Golf*, 1903

DWARFING THE INTELLECT

Excessive golfing dwarfs the intellect. And is this to be wondered at when we consider that the more fatuously vacant the mind is, the better for play. It has long been observed that absolute idiots ignorant whether they are playing two more or one off two, play steadiest. An uphill game does not make them press, nor victory within their grasp render them careless. Alas! We cannot all be idiots. Next to the idiotic, the dull unimaginative mind is the best for golf. In a professional competition I would prefer to back the sallow, dull-eyed fellow with a 'quid' in his cheek, rather than any more eager-looking champion. The poetic temperament is the worst for golf. It dreams of brilliant drives, iron shots laid dead, and long putts held, whilst in real golf success waits for him who takes care of the foozles and leaves the fine shots to take care of themselves.

Sir Walter Simpson, *The Art of Golf*, 1887

CRACKING

In well nigh every golf match which is at all a close one there is almost inevitably some one notable turning point, a crisis at which the golfing quality is put to its severest test. In the case of two golfers evenly pitted, it is most interesting to watch. After the first few holes are over there will be a ding-dong, give-and-take contest, in which the luck of the green will give now one and now the other a quickly passing advantage. They fight on neck and neck, the match draws nearer its conclusion, and still the balance hangs even. The excitement grows constantly; they are passing through the crucial test, then one or the other, in the expressive golfing parlance, 'cracks'. He plays badly, just because it is the moment at which he most wants to play his best; it has become a test of *morale*, rather than of mere eye and muscle. And the moment the one 'cracks' he is done for, the other gains confidence; the intensity of the strain has passed for him and it is scarcely in human nature that the golfer who has 'cracked' at the crucial moment can pull himself together, even if there were yet time.

Horace Hutchinson, *Golf*, Badminton Library, 1890

ON NOT KNOWING THYSELF

It takes long, long experience to convince a golfer that he must give up all the pleasures arising from a shot, except that caused by results, if he is to drive far and sure. Imitating one's own style is only less bad than copying a neighbour's. 'Know thyself' may be good philosophy; it is bad golf. Some players remain with the marks of sensation-hunting on their style for life.

For instance *A* makes himself knock-kneed when he addresses the ball. Once, long ago, when he drove a beauty, there was a feeling of gripping the ground with the balls of his big toes. If you question him warily, he will tell you the year in which, and the hole at which, the sweet shot was made that he has grown knock-

kneed in endeavouring to repeat. *B* sits down, because once, when he had a habit of
falling forward (very likely he now falls back) it restored his game. *C* turns in his toes
because it cured him of swaying his body. Of course, it was stopping swaying, not
standing like a crab, which restored his driving, but he did not know at the time
what he was doing wrong, and so he has made a fetish of his toe, which he thinks is
the God of driving. I know a golfer who does all these things, and a good many
more. In his case they have long ceased to have any meaning or effect upon his play.
They are left like labels adhering to our travelling bags – records of former trips.

Sir Walter Simpson, *The Art of Golf*, 1887

CHARACTER FORMING

Few games show the character of a person more than does that of golf, although
all, more or less, afford some index to those who are attentively looking on. A boy,
when playing, should endeavour to keep a watch over himself as much as on all
other occasions, and he should especially endeavour to practise the very important
duty of restraining his temper. Boys are too apt to fancy that they may say and do
what they like, and often they abuse each other, and make use of language of
which, it is to be hoped, they would be ashamed when out of the playground.

William H. G. Kingston, *Ernest Bracebridge or Schoolboy Days*, 1860

The modern-day army of cameramen 'attentively looking on' during the 1989 Open at Troon.

HINTS ON MATCHPLAY

How often does it not happen that you are playing two more, and think it necessary to hole in less than the perfect number to secure a half. You make an effort, fail, lose a shot more; which shot, not the two more, it turns out, costs you the hole. Everybody knows that to press a drive will not add to its length; but it is not equally acknowledged that extra mental pressure for an approach or a putt is worse than useless. The supposed necessity for pressing is born of too much respect for the enemy. Because they have got the best of you for the moment and played the hole perfectly up to a certain point, they are credited with being infallible, and you see no chance of their going into a bunker or taking four to hole off an iron. It is scarcely ever politic to count the enemy's chickens before they are hatched... A secret disbelief in the enemy's play is very useful for match play.

Sir Walter Simpson, *The Art of Golf*, 1887

COMMENTS ON GOLF

Up to this time golf has made little way in the United States. It is occasionally played in Canada, although even there it has not assumed the importance of a regular department of sports. It is a game that demands at once the utmost physical development upon the part of the player as well as a considerable amount of skill, and it arouses the interest only of those who go into sports for the love of action. It is far from being a 'dude' game. No man should attempt to play golf who has not good legs to run with and good arms to throw with, as well as a modicum of brain power to direct his play. It is also, by the nature of the game itself, a most aristocratic exercise, for no man can play at golf who has not a servant at command to assist him. It is probable that no sport exists in the world to-day or ever did exist in which the services of a paid assistant are an essential as in this national game of Scotland. The truth is that the servant is as essential to the success of the game as the player himself.

To play golf properly there is needed a very large expanse of uncultivated soil, which is not too much broken up by hills. A few knolls and gulleys more or less assist to make the game more interesting. In Scotland it is played generally upon the east coast, where the links are most extensive. Having selected a field, the first thing necessary is to dig a small hole, perhaps one foot or two feet deep and about four inches in diameter. Beginning with this hole a circle is devised that includes substantially the whole of the links. About once in 500 yards of this circle another hole is dug. If the grounds selected cannot include so large a circle as this, the holes may be put at as short a distance as 100 yards from each other; but the best game is played when the field is large enough to include holes at a distance of 500 yards

apart. The game then may be played by two or four persons. If by four, two of
them must be upon the same side.

There are eleven implements of the game, the most important of which is the
ball. This is made of gutta percha and is painted white. It weighs about two ounces
and is just small enough to fit comfortably into the holes dug in the ground. Still it
should not be so large that it cannot be taken out with ease. The other ten
implements are the tools of the players. Their names are as follows: the playing
club, long spoon, mud spoon, short spoon, baffing spoon, driving putter, putter,
sand iron, club and track iron. Each of these is about four feet long, the entire
length of which in general consists of a wooden handle. The head is spliced on,
and may be either metal or wood. The handle, as a rule, is made of hickory
covered with leather.

At the beginning of play each player places his ball at the edge of a hole which
has been designated as a starting point. When the word has been given to start he
bats his ball as accurately as possible towards the next hole which is either 100 or
500 yards distant. As soon as it is started in the air he runs forward in the direction
which the ball has taken, and his servant, who is called a 'caddy' runs after him with
all the other nine tools in his arms. If the player is expert or lucky he bats the ball so
that it falls within a few feet or inches even of the next hole in the circle. His
purpose is to put the ball in the next hole, spoon it out and drive it forward to the
next further one before his opponent can accomplish the same end. The province of
the 'caddy' in the game is to follow his master as closely as possible, generally at a
dead run, and be ready to hand him whichever implement of the game the master
calls for, as the play may demand. For instance the ball may fall in such a way that it
is lodged an inch or two above the ground, having fallen in thick grass. The player,
rushing up to it, calls on his 'caddy' for a baffing spoon, and having received it from
the hands of his servant he bats the ball with the spoon in the direction of the hole.
An inviolable rule of the game is that no player shall touch the ball from one limit of
the circle to the other with his hands. All play must be done with the tools.

In this the caddy really gets about as much exercise out of the sport as his
master, and he must be so familiar with the tools of the game that he can hand out
the right implement at any moment when it is called for. If the player has
succeeded in throwing or pushing his ball into a hole, his opponent must wait until
he has succeeded in spooning it out before he begins to play. Obedience to this rule
obviates any dispute as to the order in which a man's points are to be made. For if
one player has his ball in a hole and his opponent has his within an inch or two of
it, he must wait before he plays until the first player has gotten his ball clear of it
and thrown it towards the next hole. Following this general plan the players go
entirely about the circle, and in a large field this may involve a run of several miles.
If the ball is thrown beyond the hole, it must be returned to it and carefully
spooned out again. The aim of the sport is not necessarily to complete the circle as
quickly as possible. There are no codified rules according to which the game is

played. As a general custom the players make the entire circuit of the circle and the one who gets his ball in the hole at which they began first wins the game. Nevertheless it is sometimes agreed that the game shall be won by him who makes the largest number of holes within a given number of minutes, say twenty or thirty. In either case the principle of the game remains the same; and if partners are playing, it simply means that if *A* strikes a ball and *B* is his partner, *B* must run forward and make the next play, and *A* must run after him and make the next, and so on, while *D* and *C*, who are on the other side, are doing the same thing. In this partnership game there is actually more exercise to the players than in the single game and the servants or 'caddies' are equally busy.

One spectator getting caught up in the action during the 1985 Ryder Cup after the ball had been 'driven in a very contrary direction'.

Spectators sometimes view games of golf, but as a rule they stand far off, for the nature of the implements employed is such that a ball may be driven in a very contrary direction to that which the player wishes, and therefore may fall among the spectators and cause some temporary discomfort. Moreover it would require considerable activity upon the part of the spectators to watch the play in golf, for they would have to run around and see how every hole was gained, from one end of the game to the other. There may be as many as thirty spectators at one game, but seldom more, and a good game is frequently played without any at all.

The principal qualifications for the game are steady nerve and eye and good

judgment and force with an added ability to avoid knolls and sand-pits which, in *A modern-day*
the technical terms of the Scotch game, are called hazards. *Alexander M'Kellar?*

It is not a game which would induce men of elegance to compete in, but those *Jaime Ortiz Patino,*
who have strong wind and good muscle may find it a splendid exercise for their *the very much*
abilities, and plenty of chance to emulate each other in skill and physical endeavour. *hands-on owner of*
the Valderrama Golf

The Philadelphia Times, 24 February, 1889 *Club.*

ALEXANDER M'KELLAR

Alexander M'Kellar was probably the most enthusiastic golfer who ever lived. He
spent the whole day on Bruntsfield Links, Edinburgh, and at night would practise
putting by lamplight. Even in winter, if the snow was frozen, he would be seen
enjoying his round alone if he could not persuade any one to join him. His
absorbing predilection for the game annoyed his wife, and one day she tried to put
him to blush by carrying his dinner and nightcap to the links. She arrived at a
moment when M'Kellar was hotly engaged, and, failing to see the satire of his
wife, he observed she might wait if she chose, for at present he had not time for
dinner. He died at Edinburgh in 1813.

Golfer's Handbook, 1939

PART TWO

A ROYAL AND
VERY ANCIENT GAME

Introduction

The origins of golf are shrouded in mystery. One theory is that it began on the frozen canals of Holland and was introduced into Scotland by merchantmen plying their trade between the two countries in the 15th century. While another offers the possibility that golf began in England and was brought north in ancient times by the Romans. With no conclusive evidence to support either theory, the actual date when golfers first took up their clubs and ventured on to the links remains buried in the distant past.

The royal connection. The Duke of York, later George VI, hits the opening drive at Richmond Park Golf Club in 1925, watched by J.H. Taylor (far left).

Although Scotland is widely credited as being the home of golf, its claim is based on long tradition rather than hard historical fact. It is certain that while the game may have been introduced from outside, golf itself took root and flourished on the windswept east coast during the mid-1400s. With golf actively interfering with King James II's attempts to enforce compulsory archery practice on the common people, the game remained banned for almost a century. Golf being the game it is, the ban was made obsolete less than a century later because King James IV of Scotland had taken it up himself.

After royalty came the Church. With strong opposition over the next two hundred years, on moral grounds, the game was fortunate to have survived up to the mid-18th century and the forming of the first recognised golfing societies. With the links of St Andrews, Leith and Bruntsfield echoing to the sound of leather ball on long-nose wood, golf had truly become the national game of Scotland. Played by noble and commoner alike, golf began to attract the attention of wordsmiths and soon its pleasures were being eulogised for all the world to read about.

The first work entirely devoted to the joys of the game was Thomas Mathison's heroic-comical poem, 'The Golf'. Published in 1743, it addressed the growing interest in golf during that time and set a trend which has continued up to this very day. Proving a constant source of inspiration to writers and essayists alike, this section deals with the historic nature of golf. With items by Tobias Smollett, Horace Hutchinson and Garden G. Smith among others, it details all aspects of the game from the birth of the first organised societies, to developments in early golfing equipment. Plotting a course through golf history, it offers an invaluable insight into the rich tapestry of early golf.

GOLF

In Scotland the popular game is called Golf. It is a game that was probably played by the Romans, and in the reign of Edward III, it was called by the Latin term, *Cambuca*. It is played by two or more persons, armed with a straight-handled ash bat, the lower part of which is slightly curved. The object of the game is to drive a small, hard ball into certain holes in the ground, and he who soonest accomplishes this wins the game. It is commonly played in the winter time, sometimes on the ice. Great amusement is created by this game, when a number of players engage in it. The Scotchmen residing in London have a Golf Club; and at certain times of the year they meet at Blackheath and elsewhere, dressed in their national costume, and a very picturesque sight such a meeting is. It was at this game that Prince Henry, son of James I, used to amuse himself; in the beginning of the 17th century it was, consequently, a very fashionable game among the nobility and their initiators.

Oliver Optic, *Sports and Pastimes for in-doors and out*, 1862

Mary, Queen of Scots, at St Andrews in 1563. She is generally acknowledged as the first woman golfer.

KATHARINE OF ARAGON

Queen Katharine to Cardinal Wolsey in 1513, when Henry VIII was invading France:
Master Almoner, from hence I have nothing to write to you but that you be not so busy in this war as we be here incumbered with it. I mean that touching my own

concerns, for going further, when I shall not so often hear from the King, And all his subjects be very glad. I thank God to be busy with the golf, for they take it for pastime; my heart is very good to it, and I am horribly busy making standards, banners and bagets.

Rev John Kerr, *The Golf Book of East Lothian*, 1896

SIX CLUBS

Of the clubs there are six sorts used by proficients; viz. The *common club*, when the ball lies on the ground; the *scraper* and *half-scraper*, when in long grass; the *spoon* when in a hollow; the *heavy iron club*, when it lies deep among the stones or mud; and the *light iron club*, when on the surface of shingle or sandy ground. All these clubs are tapered at the part that strikes the ball; they are also faced with horn, and loaded with lead.

Hoyles' Games, Improved New Edition, 1816

HUGH PHILP – THE STRADIVARIUS OF GOLF

The wooden clubs in use by our ancestors of the time of the St Andrews' Museum, would seem to have been of a stubborn, stout, inflexible nature, bulldog-headed. Then arose a great master club-maker, one Hugh Philp by name, who wondrously refined golf-club nature. Slim and elegant, yet, as we of these days would say, of but insufficient power are the specimens of his art which have descended to us. His true specimens, it should be said, for there is many a club boasting Hugh Philp as its creator which that craftsman never saw – nor can we expect it would have been otherwise, since it is a matter of common report, that at least two subsequent club-makers had a 'Hugh Philp' stamp with which upon the head of the club they would imprint a blatant forgery. The golfing connoisseur will inspect the time-matured head of the old putter which claims Philp as its father with as cultured and microscopic a criticism as the dilettante love, of Stradivarius or the Amati will bestow upon their magic works.

Horace Hutchinson, *Golf*, The Badminton Library, 1890

THE CHARACTER OF PHILP

The only clubmaker was Hugh Philp. It is questionable if any other – whether before or since his time – has shaped and set a club better than he did. Hugh was a

Famous club-maker Tom Williamson, a professional at Nottingham Golf Club, with his staff. Note the iron-headed clubs waiting to be gripped with leather.

dry-haired man, rather gruff to strangers, but quite the reverse to those who knew him, with a fund of dry caustic humour, but withal a kind heart. If a man, after a match, went to him complaining of a club, Hugh would merely say 'You'll hae lost your match' and conversely with the jubilant... When I played at St Andrews with Hugh Philp (a good player and deadly at the short game) he used to ask me for one of my leaded balls. They were, however, severe upon clubs, the fairest-struck ball often breaking the head through the centre. Many of Philp's fine clubs have been broken in this way, and when I complained of rotten wood he would answer, 'Hoo the deevil can a man mak' clubs to stand against lead?'

H. Thomas Peter, *Reminiscences of Golf and Golfers*

BALANCE NOT BEAUTY

I am afraid players pay too much attention to appearance and too little to balance. A club may have a most finished appearance, but nevertheless be a terrible sinner in the outward guise of a complete saint. Many and many a club has been sold on its looks alone, irrespective of its balance. Purchasers are apt to come to the conclusion that

'Many a club has been sold on its looks alone.' Ian Woosnam's club really is as long as it looks.

an instrument of such outward beauty cannot possibly be an indifferent weapon, and notwithstanding many warnings in the past that beauty is but skin deep, even when applied to such a prosaic thing as a golf club, they cannot resist the temptation of adding it to their collection, possibly not without some misgivings, as they probably have a lurking suspicion in their minds that all is not really well. But the apparent beauty of outline invariably overrules their better judgement in the end and another proud but useless beauty is added to their stock. A great number of these little tragedies happen after a day's golf, when daylight has failed, and the purchaser views the goods under the glamour of artificial light. It is the most difficult thing in the world to judge a club by gaslight as it seems to throw out in bold relief the virtues of the instrument, and draw a veil over its defects. I have many times known a player purchase a club when the sun has gone down and almost fail to recognise his purchase by the broad light of day, and he ruefully remarks: 'Somehow or other this club does not seem quite the same as it did last night; perhaps I have got the wrong one.' But it is in truth the same weapon he had been so keen on the night before. I have been through the sad experience myself and so can speak feelingly; but I have learnt my lesson, and nowadays I never buy a club except in daylight, and moreover I try to avoid buying a club within the precincts of a domicile or a clubhouse as clubs have a habit of appearing at their very best when reposing for inspection on a carpet or even an oilcloth. On a thick carpet in particular they have a most alluring appearance, and if I were in the business I should certainly cover the floor of my show-room with a thick heavy carpet. The carpet might cost money, but I would possibly get rid of many ugly ducklings thereby. The only place really to judge a club is on the turf itself in a good light.

H. H. Hilton, *The Royal & Ancient Game of Golf,* 1912

THE ANATOMY OF A CLUB

Nearly everyone carries a play club, an instrument consisting of many parts. It has no legs, but a shaft instead. It has, however, a toe. Its toe is at the end of its face, close to its nose, which is not on its face. Although it has no body, it has a sole. It has a neck, a head, and clubs also have horns. They always have a whipping, but this has nothing to do directly with striking the ball. There is little expression in the face of a club. It is usually wooden; sometimes however it has a leather face. Clubs, without being clothed, occasionally have lead buttons, but never any button-holes. Club's heads are sometimes black, sometimes yellow, but colour is not due to any racial difference. From this description it will be easy to understand without a diagram what a club is like.

Spoons in some respects resemble clubs. Their faces are somewhat more open. There are long, short and mid spoons, so called according to the length of the spoon. Brassies differ from spoons and play clubs in that they have brass bottoms which are screwed on.

Irons and cleeks have no sole. Their toes and noses are one and the same thing. They have iron faces. They are never whipped. They have sockets instead of necks. Their mode of locomotion is called 'approaching'. This is a short swinging gait and sometimes, like play clubs, they drive, but no kind of club ever walks. There are different kinds of irons. A driving iron is used when it is too far to go without doing so. Lofting irons are more light-headed; they look like their work, but do not always do it. Cleeks are cleeks; they are not marked out from their creation for special uses. You may carry a driving and an approaching cleek, and a cleek for putting; but if someone steals your set, or if you die, your putting cleek may be used for driving etc., etc.

Then there are putters. A good one ought to have the name 'Philp' stamped on it by somebody who must not tell you that he did it himself, as it must have belonged to someone else before you got it – either an old golfer who is dead (no matter whether he was a good holer-out or not) or else to a professional. No golfer with any self-respect uses a putter which he has bought new out of a shop for four shillings. The niblick is too vulgar-looking for description in a polite treatise like this. He is a good fellow, however, ever ready to get you out of a hole.

Sir Walter Simpson, *The Art of Golf*, 1887

A GOLF RETROSPECT BY A GUTTA BALL

It must be nearly eight years since, after being badly sliced off the tee, I was lost in the long grass going to the third hole on the most sporting nine-hole inland course in the United Kingdom. There I have remained until the present day, and, ever observant, many things have interested me. I have noticed, though, in my days it took two full wooden shots to reach the green; it is now reached by a drive and an iron, and if I had not lately been joined by a kindly, though somewhat overbearing, 'Haskell', I should have attributed it to the much improved forearm and wrist-work of the present golfer in timing the ball off the tee. My friend the 'Haskell', though much mutilated, was able to explain to me that owing to his thin skin and rubber surrounded heart he had a much further carry off the tee, and this, reluctantly, I had to believe.

I have seen pass me all these years good players and bad players, and good golfers and bad golfers. I have seen the local parson toiling on, taking serenely ten strokes to a five hole, and yet perfectly happy. I have seen, after a pulled drive of R. Maxwell's in the ditch, Johnnie Laidley, with turned-up collar, playing a brilliant recovery on the green.

I have seen that famous cricketer, R. E. Foster, hole our second hole with his tee shot; and quite lately I have seen our worthy captain, on the top of his game, lower the colours of the present amateur champion. And if one day I am found, my wish is to be taken to our dear old Scotch pro. And perhaps he will wash me clean and place me on the mantelpiece of his workshop, and point me out as a relic of golf of the olden days.

Badminton Magazine, 1899

INTRODUCTION OF THE GUTTY

Golf was rendered expensive in those days, not by the clubs, which were cheaper then than now, but by the balls. Their prime cost was high, and their durability not

A long-nose putter made by Frank Bell (c. 1875) pictured with an ancient feather ball (c. 1845) stamped 'Saddell'.

great. On a wet day, for example, a ball soon became soaked, soft and flabby; so that a new one had to be used at every hole in a match of any importance. Or, on the other hand, a 'top' by an iron in a bunker might cut it through. This I have frequently seen occur.

The making of first-class feather balls was almost a science. For the benefit of the uninitiated, I shall endeavour to explain the operation. The leather was of untanned bull's hide. Two round pieces for the ends, and a stripe for the middle were cut to suit the weight wanted. These were properly shaped, after being sufficiently softened, and firmly sewed together – a small hole being of course left, through which the feathers might be afterwards inserted. But, before stuffing, it was through this little hole that the leather itself had to be turned outside in, so that the seams should be inside – an operation not without difficulty. The skin was then placed in a cup-shaped stand (the worker having the feathers in an apron in front of him), and the actual stuffing done with a crutch-handled steel rod, which the maker placed under his arm. And very hard work, I may add, it was. Thereafter, the aperture was closed, and firmly sewed up; and this outside seam was the only one visible. When I say this, I of course refer to balls when new. Veterans showed the effects of service in open seams, with feathers out-looking; and on a wet day the water could be seen driven off in showers from a circle of protruding feathers, as from a spray-producer. A ball perhaps started a 'twenty-eight', and ended a forty pounder.

The introduction of gutta-percha balls effected a complete revolution. Their cost was small, their durability great. I believe I may with justice claim the credit of having first brought them to the notice of the golfing world, and this at the Spring Meeting of the Innerleven Club in 1848. The previous month, when on my way home from a two years' stay in France (where, by the way, golf was then unknown), I chanced to see in the window of a shop down a stair in St David Street, Edinburgh, a placard bearing the words – 'New golf balls for sale.'

I found them different from anything I had seen before; and was told by the shopman they were 'guttie-perkies'.

'Guttie-perkie! What's that?' I asked; for I had never heard of it.

'It's a kin'o' gum like indiarubber.'

'What kind of balls does it make?'

'I ken naething aboot that – best try yin yoursel'!'

I bought one for a shilling. It was not painted, but covered with a sort of 'size', which, after some practice with my brother James, who was a good golfer, I saw reason to scrape off.

I then determined to try it upon the Innerleven Links, against Mr David Wallace, a golfer with whom I often played, and who always beat me. I noticed that after I had 'teed', he looked at my ball with great curiosity; so I told him its history and the result of my experiments; and away we went. The upshot of our day's play was, that I beat him by thirteen holes – a thrashing, he said, such as he had never had in his life. However, he, too, soon took to the 'guttas'; and many a beating he gave me afterwards. Still, I was much more on an equality with him than before.

I won the silver medal against him in April, 1848; and it was at that meeting I showed the new ball to Allan Roberston and Tom Morris. It was the first time either had ever seen a 'gutta'. I told them of its great superiority to 'feathers', and that the days of the latter were numbered; but Allan would not believe it. At my request, he tried the new ball; but instead of hitting it fairly; struck it hard on the top in a way to make it duck (which, by the way, no one could do more deftly than Allan).

'Bah!' he said; 'that thing'll never flee!'

I, however, struck it fairly, and, to Allan's disgust, away it flew beautifully!

For a long time Allan persisted in this opposition to 'guttas'. He has often told me, when I wanted him as partner in a foursome, that he would not play unless I used feather balls – a condition to which I, of course, acceded. At last, however, even Allan had to yield. He not only began to make them (as many others had by that time done): but played with them.

Tom Morris, on the other hand, took the whole thing in a different way. His customers informed him that 'feathers' were doomed; he at once made 'guttas', and very successfully. Nay, if I remember rightly, his difference with Allan on this subject led to their separation.

For long I made my own balls, and at small cost. The only point in which 'guttas' were at a disadvantage, as compared with 'feathers', was that they did not hold their course well in high wind, specially a side one. After some scheming and experiment, my brother and I succeeded in inserting and fixing lead securely in the centre of the ball, so that it putted accurately.

Nearly all the medals I gained were won with leaded balls; and I used them regularly until my stock was exhausted. (The making of them ceased at my brother's death.) They were well known at that time; and when I played St Andrews with Hugh Philp (a good player and deadly at the short game) he used to ask me for one of my leaded balls.

Other players, again, used to lead their balls by rolling them when warm in lead filings; but as these were on the surface, they fell out when the ball was struck, and gave it a very unsightly appearance. That plan was inferior to ours.

I may mention that for a considerable time I played with unpainted balls under the impression that they flew better; but there was, of course, the draw-back that they were difficult to find.

H. Thomas Peter, *Golfing Reminiscences by an Old Hand*, 1890

THE IMPORTANCE OF STYLE

It is of the first importance that a golfer should have a good style of play, these words being here used as including grip of club, stance, and swing. One frequently hears it said, 'What does my style signify provided I can play a good game?' To this I would reply, 'In the majority of cases it is hardly possible to play a good game unless you have a good style.' It is also said that if the best golfers be closely watched no two of them have the same style, and which among all these styles is the correct one? My answer to this is that there are few crack players who have not a good style, and that although there may be, and undoubtedly are, many whose styles are different in detail, they are fundamentally the same – they are all modelled on the recognised lines. There are, however, among the followers of every game men whose play can hardly be excelled, and who yet violate the canons of style. Such players have been termed geniuses, and a few are to be found among the ranks of golfers; but I would further say that these are the exceptions that prove the rule. The imitators of geniuses seldom attain to any perfection, and generally find it difficult to reach mediocrity. For geniuses no rules can be laid down – their success justifies their play, but only their success. Failure would heap on their heads deserved ridicule.

I would recommend all golfers to model their styles upon the recognised lines that have stood the test of decades of play at the hands of the best amateurs and professionals. If anyone finds himself to be a genius, he can easily carve out his own peculiar style, and will be none the worse, but probably much the better, for having begun upon the orthodox lines.

Willie Park, *The Game of Golf*, 1896

HOW TO GO ABOUT BUYING A PUTTER

If you wish a good putter, you will hardly expect to find one in a clubmaker's ready-made stock, far less in a toyshop or a tobacconist's window. The putter must be sought for with care and not hastily, for she is to be the friend, be it hoped, of many years. First, then, find out a workman of repute as a maker of putters – and in these days of 'reach-me-down' clubs there are few such artists – and, having found him, proceed warily. It will never do to go and order him to make you a first-class club for your match next morning; you would probably receive only the work of an apprentice. Wait your time and you will find the great man about his shop, or on his doorstep at the dinner hour, and may remark to him that the day is fine; this will be a safe opening, even though rain be falling in torrents, for it will give him the idea that you are a simple fellow and so throw him off his guard.

If a half-empty pipe lies beside him, offer him a cigar, and mention that you are afraid that it is not as good as you would have wished, being the last of the box, at the same time giving him to understand that another box is expected that evening. The cigar having been accepted and lighted, you may, in course of conversation, allude to a very fine putter made by a rival clubmaker which, you will tell your friend, is being much talked about and copied. This will be almost certainly a winning card to play, for there is much jealousy among the profession, and as likely as not the remark will be made that So-and-so – naming the rival maker – has about as much idea of fashioning a putter as he has of successfully solving the problem of aerial navigation. Do not press the matter to a conclusion, but meet your man again in similar manner, this time carelessly holding in your hand the club which you have long felt was the cause of the success of some distinguished player. Almost seem to hide it from the clubmaker, and he will be sure to ask to see it, and probably volunteer to make you one on the same lines with slight improvements of his own. In time you will get your putter, and it will probably be a good one; in any case it will be good enough to resell if it does not suit you, which is always a point to be considered.

John L. Low, *Concerning Golf*, 1903

JUSTICE IN GOLF

As a general principle, at every hole, except on the putting green where it brings its own reward, a bad shot should be followed by a bad lie, and a good shot should be correspondingly rewarded by a good one. Now it is impossible, at every hole, to provide a fitting punishment for every kind of bad shot. If this were done the soul

Bernhard Langer receiving a 'fitting punishment for every kind of bad shot' during the 1981 Benson and Hedges International Open at Fulford. He made a famous escape.

of the stoutest-hearted golfer would quail at the number of hazards with which the prospect from the tee would bristle, and all the pleasurable excitement and charm of the game would disappear. But there is one kind of bad stroke which by universal consent must be summarily punished, whenever and wherever it is perpetrated, and that is a 'topped shot'. The reasons for this are obvious. The shot has been missed and missed badly, but on hard ground or against a wind, a topped ball will sometimes run as far, or even further than a clean hit one, and the player will suffer no disadvantage from his mistake. Wherefore, in making your first tee, select a spot some sixty yards in front of which a yawning bunker stretches right across the course, and if it be so narrow or so shallow, that a topped ball will jump over it or run through it, dig it wider and deeper, so that all balls crossing its jaws will inevitably be swallowed up. If no bunker is to be had, a pond will do equally well, or a railway or a hedge or a wall – anything in short that is impassable.

In the case of our first hole, in burning and hacking a course of 60 or 80 yards through the gorse and grubbing up the roots, all holes will have to be filled up and returfed; but the man who tops his tee shot should be remembered, and for his sake, and for the encouragement and protection of those who do better, you will do well to leave a solid belt of the gorse all across the course, about 60 yards from the tee.

A long driver, when he hits his ball clean, will carry some 150 to 170 yards, and a less powerful player some 130 to 150 yards. From 100 to 130 yards, then, from the tee, there should be another hazard of some sort to catch balls which, though good enough to escape the primal punishment for topped balls, have yet been hit with considerable inaccuracy. Beyond the second hazard, the ground should be good for 80 or 100 yards, but guarding the hole again, there should be another hazard which the player will have to loft over before reaching the putting green. In addition the course may be garnished on either side according to the taste or fancy of the maker, with other hazards, to catch crooked balls, and also beyond the hole to punish those that are hit too strongly, but 'blind hazards' i.e. hazards which are not visible to the player, such as sunk ditches or holes, should either be rendered visible or filled up.

Garden G. Smith, *The World of Golf,* (The Isthmian Library), 1898

THE LINKS OF LEITH

Hard by, in the fields called the Links, the citizens of Edinburgh divert themselves at a game called Golf, in which they use a curious kind of bats tipped with horn, and small elastic balls of leather, stuffed with feathers, rather less than tennis balls, but of a much harder consistence. These they strike with such force and dexterity from one hole to another, that they will fly to an incredible distance. Of this diversion the Scots are so fond, that, when the weather will permit, you may see a multitude of all

Golfing on Leith Links, c. 1850. Once the most famous course in Scotland, it is now little more than a city centre park in Edinburgh.

ranks, from the senator of justice to the lowest tradesman, mingled together, in their shirts, and following the balls with the utmost eagerness. Among others, I was shown one particular set of golfers, the youngest of whom was turned of four-score. They were all gentlemen of independent fortunes, who had amused themselves with this pastime for the best part of a century without having ever felt the least alarm from sickness or disgust; and they never went to bed without having each the best part of a gallon of claret in his belly. Such uninterrupted exercise, co-operating with the keen air from the sea, must, without all doubt, keep the appetite always on edge, and steel the constitution against all the common attacks of distemper.

Tobias Smollett, *The Expedition of Humphrey Clinker*, 1771

BRUNTSFIELD LINKS

Bruntsfield Links, 29th Jan 1842. A very large party dined at Cork's and the evening was spent with more than stereotyped happiness, harmony and hilarity. A number of matches were made. Mr S. Aitken (not of course when 'madness ruled the hour') pledged himself, if and when Deacon Scott married, to present to the Club half-a-dozen of wine, and the like quantity to the object (lovely of course) of his choice! This happy meeting, though 'through many a bout of linked sweetness long drawn out', partook of the transitory nature of all earthly things, and, as one of our poets says – broke up!

Minutes of the Bruntsfield Links Golf Club

GOLF ON BRUNTSFIELD LINKS

No part of Edinburgh has a more agreeable southern exposure than those large open spaces round the Meadows (which we have described elsewhere) and Bruntsfield Links, which contribute both to their health and amenity.

The latter have long been famous as a playground for the ancient and national game of golf, and strangers who may be desirous of enjoying it, are usually supplied with clubs and assistants at the old Golf Tavern, that overlooks the breezy and grassy scene of operations, which affords space for the members of no less than six golf clubs, viz:– the Burghers, instituted 1735; the Honourable Company of Edinburgh, instituted prior to 1744; the Bruntsfield, instituted 1761; the Allied Golfing Club, instituted 1856; the Warrender, instituted 1858; and the St Leonards, instituted 1857. Each of these is presided over by a captain, and the usual playing costume is a scarlet coat, with the facings and gilt buttons of the club.

To dwell at length on the famous game of golf is perhaps apart from the nature of this work, and yet, as these Links have been for ages the scene of that old sport, a few notices of it may be acceptable.

It seems somewhat uncertain at what precise period golf was introduced into Scotland; but some such game, called cambuca, was not unknown in England during the reign of Edward III, as we may learn from Strutt's 'Sports and Pastimes', but more probably he refers to that known as Pall Mall. Football was prohibited by Act of the Scottish Parliament in 1424, as interfering with the more necessary science of archery, but the statute makes no reference to golf, while it is specially mentioned in later enactments, in 1457 and 1471, under James III; but still it seems to have thriven, and in the accounts of the Lord High Treasurer, under James IV, the following entries are found:–

1503, Feb. 3. Item to the King to play at the Golf with the Erle of Bothwile... xlijs.

1503, Feb. 4. Item to Golf Clubbes and Ballis to the King... ixs.

1503, Feb. 22. Item, xij Golf Balls to the King... iiijs.

1506. Item, the 28th day of Julii for ij Golf Clubbes to the King... ijs.

During the reign of James VI the business of club making had become one of some importance, and by a letter, dated Holyrood, 4th April, 1603, William Mayne, Bowyer, burgess of Edinburgh, is appointed maker of bows, arrows, spears, and clubs to the King. From thenceforward the game took a firm hold of the people as a national pastime, and it seems to have been a favourite one with Henry, Duke of Rothesay, and with the great Marquis of Montrose, as the many entries in his 'Household Book' prove. 'Even kings themselves,' says a writer in the *Scots Magazine* for 1792, 'did not decline the princely sport; and it will not be displeasing to the Society of Edinburgh Golfers to be informed that the two last crowned heads that ever visited this country (Charles I and James VII) used to practise golf on the Links of Leith, now occupied by the society for the same purpose.'

In 1744 the city gave a silver club, valued at £15, to be played for on the 1st of April annually by the Edinburgh Company of Golfers, the victor to be styled captain for the time, and to append a gold or silver medal to the club, bearing his name and date of victory. The Honourable Company was incorporated by a charter from the magistrates in 1800, and could boast of the most illustrious Scotsmen of the day among its members. Until the year 1792 St Andrews had a species of monopoly in the manufacture of golf balls. They are small and hard, and of old were always stuffed with feathers. The clubs are from three to four feet long. 'The heads are of brass,' says Dr Walker, in a letter to the famous Dr Carlyle of Inveresk; 'and the face with which the ball is struck is perfectly smooth, having no inclination, such as might have a tendency to raise the ball from the ground. The game may be played by any number, either in parties against each other, or each person for himself, and the contest is to hole the course in the fewest strokes.'

'Far!' or 'Fore!' is the signal cry before the ball is struck, to warn loiterers or spectators; and 'Far and Sure!' is a common motto with golf clubs.

Topham, an English traveller in Scotland in 1775, in describing the customs of the Scots, makes the *summit* of Arthur's Seat and other high hills round Edinburgh the favourite places for playing golf!

In virtue of a bet in 1798, Mr Scales of Leith, and Mr Smellie, a printer, were selected to perform the curious feat of driving a ball from the south-east corner of the Parliament Square over the weathercock of St Giles's, 161 feet from the base of the church. They were allowed the use of six balls each. These all went considerably higher than the vane, and were found in the Advocate's Close, on the north side of the High Street.

Duncan Forbes, the Lord President, was so fond of golf that he was wont to play on the sands of Leith when the Links were covered with snow. Kay gives us a portrait of a famous old golfer, Andrew McKellar, known as the 'Cock o' the Green', in the act of striking the ball. This enthusiast spent entire days on Bruntsfield Links, club in hand, and was often there by night too, playing at the 'short holes' by lantern light. Andrew died about 1813.

Bruntsfield Links and those of Musselburgh are the favourite places yet of the Edinburgh Club; but the St Andrews meetings are so numerously attended that the old city by the sea has been denominated the *Metropolis* of golfing.

In a miscellaneous collection, entitled 'Mistura Curiosa, a song in praise of golf has two verses thus:–

I love the game of golf, my boys, though there are folks in town
Who, when upon the Links they walk, delight to run it down;
But then those folks who don't love golf, of course, can't comprehend
The fond love that exists between the golfer and his friend.
For on the green the new command, that ye love one another,
Is, as a rule, kept better by a golfer than a brother;
For if he's struck, a brother's rage is not so soon appeased,
But the harder that I hit my friend, the better he is pleased.

Until the Royal Park at Holyrood was opened up, levelled, and improved, at the suggestion of the late Prince Consort, Bruntsfield Links was the invariable place for garrison reviews and field days by the troops; but neither they nor any one else can interfere with the vested rights of the golfers to play over any part of the open ground at all times.

Old & New Edinburgh, 1898

ST ANDREWS

The Course is marvellously adapted to the game. It used to be flanked by high whins for the greater part of its extent, and these formed an interesting hazard. The turf is smooth and fine; the subsoil is sandy; the surface sometimes undulating

'The Golfers – A Grand Match Played over St Andrews Links' by Charles Lees. It depicts the 1841 match between Sir David Baird and Sir Ralph Anstruther against Major Playfair and John Campbell of Saddell. (Christie's Images)

and sometimes flat. There are beautiful level putting greens, while the Course is studded with sand-pits or bunkers as golfers call them. These, with the ever-recurring hazards of whin, heather and bent all combine to give endless variety, and to adapt the Links at St Andrews to the game of golf in a way quite unsurpassed anywhere else. If there be added to its golfing charms the charms of all its surroundings – the grand history of St Andrews and its sacred memories – its delightful air – the song of its numberless larks, which nestle among the whins – the scream of the sea-birds flying overhead – the blue sea dotted with a few fishing boats – the noise of the waves and the bay of the Eden as seen from the high hole when the tide is full – the venerable towers and the broken outline of the ancient city; and in the distance the Forfarshire coast, with the range of the Sidlaws, and, further off, the Grampian hills, it may be truly said that probably no portion of ground of the same size on the whole surface of the globe has afforded so much innocent enjoyment to so many people of all ages from two to eighty-nine, and during so many generations.

James Balfour, *Reminiscences of Golf on St Andrews Links*, 1887

WESTWARD HO!

I can remember, on the question of the modern cost of golf at Westward Ho! that almost the sole expense was for clubs and balls. Nature, and a few sheep cropping the grass, which never grew long on that link's turf, did all the rest for us. I am not quite sure that we did not think we had done a very big thing – almost gone too far on the lines of luxury and precise attention to having all in perfect order – when one of the members sent to Scotland for a hole cutter.

Previous to that enormous piece of extravagance the mode had been to cut out the holes with an ancient dinner-knife, or clasp knife. Sometimes – but even this seemed a first lapse towards a precision that was almost meticulous – a gallipot was held on the ground to give a circle round which the knife should incise the turf. The holes grew and grew, in diameter, with wear, and were notched away here and there at their edges, although there was no large multitude of golfers to do the wearing away, so that a wily man, finding the putt a difficult one with a troublous little rise in the ground interposing in the direct route between him and the hole, would putt so as to try to let the ball fall in by one of those bays or notches in the edge if there were an easier putt towards the kindly welcoming entry.

There was no fixed day for the cutting of a new hole, but when the leading players on any day found one of the holes too far gone in decay to be longer endurable, he would out with his knife and cut a new hole to which he and his opponent would putt, and thereafter all who followed could putt likewise.

The site of the hole would be indicated by the feather of a rook or a gull struck into the ground at its edge, for by these simple means did these good men, our forbears, mark the situation of the holes.

In some old rules of golf – remarkably few in number compared with the elaborate code of today – you may find a provision that the ball shall be teed for the next hole not less than three, nor more than four, club lengths from the hole lately played out.

That gives you an indication of the state of original sin in which the putting greens were left, when you could do no harm to them so long as you did not tee up and take your stance and drive off nearer the hole than three club lengths.

It indicates, too, and rightly, that there were no set teeing marks. Distance from the previous hole, as stated, gave you the approximate limits within which you might tee. And as there were no teeing marks, neither were there tee boxes for sand.

The easiest and natural and usual way to get sand for the teeing of the ball was to scoop it out of the last hole played and this was the plan always followed. It had the effect, if the turf was sound so that the hole kept its edges good and was not shifted for some while, that as more and more sand was taken out the hole grew more and more profound, until it often happened that one had to lie down so as to stretch one's arm at full length in order to reach the ball at the bottom of the hole.

Once upon a time there was a rabbit which played a very remarkable practical joke upon some of us at Westward Ho! With great discrimination it refrained from any onset upon the turf in the neighbourhood of the hole which might have given warning of its presence, but made use of the hole itself as an entry providentially constructed, and dug down from the bottom of the hole nobody ever discovered how far. Of course, the result was that as party after party came to the hole they putted out but were altogether unable to retrieve the ball which had gone down into the very bowels of the earth.

It would, to be sure, have been only right and humane of the first party to whom this disaster happened to block up the floor of the hole so that the same should not befall those who came after. But each party in turn, having lost their own balls, did not see why they should go back to be laughed at by the others. Accordingly, they left the trap gaping open so that all should be taken in equally and none have the laugh over the other.

But the rabbit must have laughed at the bottom of its burrow, and probably set up a gutta-percha store on the result.

Horace Hutchinson, 'Old Memories of Westward Ho!', *The Midland Golfer*, 1914

INDIAN OFFICERS

At Westward Ho!... we had many old Indian Officers, with livers a little touched, and manners acquired in a course of years of dealing with the mild Hindoo, and because the golf ball would not obey their wishes with the same docility as the obedient Oriental, they addressed it with many strange British words which I delighted to hear and yet stranger words in Hindustani which I much regretted not to understand. But a sight that has been seen at Westward Ho! is that of a gallant Colonel stripping himself to the state in which Nature gave him to an admiring world, picking his way daintily with unshod feet over the great boulders of the Pebble Ridge, and when he came to the sea, wading out as far as possible, and hurling forth, one after the other, beyond the line of the farthest breakers the whole set of his offending clubs. That the waves and the tide were sure to bring them in again, to the delight of the salvaging caddies, made no matter to him. From him they were gone for ever and his soul was at rest.

Of course he bought a new set on the morrow, so it was all good for trade and Johnny Allan. It also afforded a splendid spectacle to an admiring gallery. Really we have lost much at Westward Ho!, even if we have gained much, by the bringing of the Clubhouse across the common. It was delightful, after golf or between the rounds, to bathe off that Ridge, or sit on it and watch the sea tumbling...

Horace Hutchinson, 'Fifty Years of Golf', *Country Life* Library, 1914

THE GOLFER'S GARB

During the last hundred and fifty years the Royal and Ancient Game has seen many changes, but in nothing has there been a greater change than in the matter of the golfer's attire. Golf was for centuries the national pastime of the Scots, but there is no evidence, literary or pictorial, that any Scot has ever worn a kilt at his national game. Yet the garb of old golf appears to us nowadays fantastic enough. In the last half of the eighteenth century the ordinary dress of the golfing 'buck' was a red coat, cut rather long, with side pockets, knee-breeches, white stockings and buckled shoes, and for headgear a broad Scottish bonnet or Tam O'Shanter. But about the end of the century considerable attention was bestowed on the question of golfing attire, and each club had its own uniform, which was *de rigueur* at all club meetings and functions. Those who appeared in ordinary civilian attire were fined in dozens of claret, which were consumed there and then, or at the first opportunity, by their outraged fellow-members. The minutes of the Royal and Ancient and Royal Aberdeen Clubs show that the old golfers were not easy to please in the cut or colour of their coats, and long debates took place on the precise details of the club uniform. Usually it consisted of a red tail-coat faced with various colours, and decorated with brass buttons bearing the arms and name or motto of the club. Sometimes the club arms were emblazoned in silk on the left breast. The Aberdeen golfers swithered for some time between red and Lincoln green, but ultimately decided on the former. The Royal and Ancient golfers were

even harder to please, and exhibited an almost feminine caprice in their choice of *Golf in top hats and* raiment. In 1780 the club coat was red with yellow buttons, but eleven of the *tails. A rare early* members, headed by the Earl of Balcarres, resolved to have 'an uniform frock, viz., *photograph showing a* a buff colour with a red cap. The coat to be half lapelled, according to a pattern *group of golfers at* produced, the button white.' Four years later it was decreed that the uniform was *Musselburgh,* to be 'a red coat with a dark blue velvet cape, with plain white buttons, with an *including Tom Morris* embroidered club and ball on each side of the cape, with two large buttons on the *Snr (seventh from* sleeves'. *left).*

This fashion apparently endured till 1820, in which year it was enacted that the uniform of the club should be a plain blue coat with the club buttons. How long this lasted is not recorded, but ultimately the club reverted to the original red colour, which was almost the universal colour until the wearing of club uniforms died out. In the tail-coat period, tall hats were worn as well as the cloth Scottish bonnets, but, except for short periods, it does not appear.

Garden G. Smith, *The Royal & Ancient Game of Golf*, 1912

THE SOCIAL SIDE

Although the old golfing societies from 1759 onwards had their annual medal meetings, they did not indulge in any other stroke-play competitions. The private match, single or foursome, was the great thing all the year round, and there is no record for nearly a hundred years of any inter-club match. The first match of this nature of which we have been able to find a record was played on Bruntsfield Links, in Edinburgh, on May 16, 1835, between teams of the Burgess Golfing Society and the Star Golf Club. The Star Club has left no other memorial of its existence. It is interesting to note that the result of this and all other early inter-club matches was calculated by the total number of *holes* won by each side, and not, as is now the fashion, by the majority of *matches* won. The leading clubs, the Honourable Company and the Royal and Ancient, never played these inter-club matches, nor do they do so now, and in this exclusiveness they have been followed by Prestwick and most of the older English clubs. The leading Scottish clubs were very close corporations, and their memberships were jealously confined to men not only of a certain social standing, but to members of certain professions and even families. The golf clique and the black ball are amongst the most ancient of golf-club institutions.

Before the first golfing societies were formed, all classes mingled freely on the links, as they did at all sports; but with the settling of the country society began to form itself into groups and coteries. So it happened in golf. The fine old Scottish 'gentleman golfer' was a great patrician in his way, and not given to condescending to men of low estate. The butcher, the baker, and the candlestick-maker might be very honest fellows, and good golfers and sportsmen, but they were by no means fit for the honourable company of the lawyers, ministers, professors, and publishers who hobnobbed with the lairds and nobility in the sacred precincts of the club. So the grand seigneurs of the game clubbed and played 'be thame selffes', and the humbler bourgeoisie 'be thame selffes', and it was to the bourgeois clubs, in which the social feeling was less exclusive, that the inter-club match owed its origin.

But if the early clubs were somewhat exclusive and unsociable in their dealings with each other, they made ample amends when assembled under their own roof-trees and round their own festive boards. The old club records are quite as full of references to the golfers' exploits at the club dinners as to their deeds on the links.

The splendid collection of old china drinking vessels formerly belonging to the Knuckle Club at Blackheath and the old Blackheath Golf Club, which is still extant, is eloquent of how largely the social and convivial element entered into golf in the old days. The ample proportions of these old drinking utensils – it is hard to find a word that will fitly express their size and business-like aspect – are positively staggering. Of course it is not to be supposed that these huge Joram Jugs represented the units of consumption on a sort of 'one man one jug' principle. They were not the actual drinking vessels, but merely the common receptacles from

Ex-caddie Auld Daw Anderson (centre) was given exclusive rights to serve golfers on the Old Course at St Andrews in the late 19th century. Because ginger beer was a favourite tipple, to this day the fourth is known as 'The Ginger Beer Hole'.

which the drinking glasses were filled and replenished according to the needs of the *convives*. But even so, there is nothing niggardly, nothing of half-measures, in their aspect. On the contrary, there is a roomy, provident, and generous look about them which suggests a doubt as to the prevalence of temperance principles amongst those who used them. Nor, indeed, was there any temperance about the matter.

It was a convivial age, when it was no discredit for a gentleman to drink to what is now deemed excess. There may have been a certain amount of etiquette as to how he carried it, but a man who could not drink his two bottles ran a fair chance of being set down as a milksop. For a guest to shirk his fair share of the enormous quantity of liquor provided was considered a breach of good manners and an abuse of hospitality. 'Drunk as a lord' was not the empty phrase it has since become; it actually represented the glorious and habitual condition of the male portion of the nobility, at any rate after dinner. But however shocking, in these temperate times, such customs may appear, it has to be remembered that the liquor so plentifully consumed was not the heady and poisonous stuff which, in smaller quantities, is fashionable to-day. It was not champagne, nor whisky, nor even beer, with which these huge beakers were filled and refilled, but light French claret, of a quality rarely to be met with nowadays, whereof it may truly be said that there was not a headache in a hogshead of it.

So much for the Joram Jugs and their contents. But what about the capacious bowls that form so conspicuous a part in this Blackheath collection? Surely they were not for claret also. No one has ever put claret in a bowl, and claret cup is quite a modern concoction. Here it is to be feared we are outside the region of extenuation, and the most ardent apologist is obliged to confess that their plain and obvious purport is Punch!

Of course, it may be conceded that the brew which filled these Titanic basins was of the best: the old Blackheath golfers, most of them city merchants, shipowners, and the like, and many of them Scots, would see to that; and it is pleasant to picture them seated round the long, black oak table while some old warrior, his jovial face wreathed in clouds of best Virginian,

'would mix the genuine stuff
As they made it long ago,
With limes which on his property
In Trinidad did grow.'

The matches and bets were made before the cloth was removed, but we can hear the toasts – not all of them, be sure, loyal to the House of Hanover – the stories, the songs, the speeches, and the fines. And, by and by, the 'gentlemen golfers' would wend their devious ways to their respective abodes, 'happy to meet, sweir to part, and happy to meet again'.

Modern golf-club dinners, with their rather formal proceedings, have little in common with the Bacchanalian orgies which our golfing sires celebrated in the more genial licence of the tavern. Whether the old golfers were better players than ourselves may be open to doubt; there can be no question of their superiority round the wassail bowl.

Garden G. Smith, *The Royal & Ancient Game of Golf*, 1912

A SCOTTISH GREETING IN KENSINGTON

Garrick was so friendly to John Home that he gave a dinner to his friends and companions at his house at Hampton, which he did but seldom. He had told us to bring golf clubs and balls that we might play at that game at Molesey Hurst. We accordingly set out in good time, six of us in a landau. As we passed through Kensington the Coldstream Regiment were changing guard, and, on seeing our clubs, they gave us three cheers in honour of a diversion peculiar to Scotland; so much does the remembrance of one's native country dilate the heart when one has been some time absent... Immediately after we arrived we crossed the river to the golfing ground, which was very good. None of the company could play but John Home and myself and Parson Black from Aberdeen.

Garrick had built a handsome temple, with a statue of Shakespeare in it, in his lower garden on the banks of the Thames, which was separated from the upper one by a high road, under which there was an archway which united the two gardens... Having observed a green mound in the garden opposite the archway, I said to our landlord, that while the servants were preparing the collation in the temple I would surprise him with a stroke at the golf, as I should drive the ball through his archway into the Thames once in three strokes. I had measured the distance with my eye in walking about the garden, and, accordingly, at the second stroke, made the ball alight in the mouth of the gateway and roll down the green slope into the river. This was so dexterous that he was quite surprised, and begged the club of me by which such a feat had been performed.

Alexander Carlyle, *Autobiography*, 1860

GOLF IN THE UNITED STATES

The main difference between golf in America and golf in England is that one is artificial and the other is natural. The climate and soil of the United States are such that they do not admit of the perfect natural courses which abound around the coast of England and Scotland. In a few places like Long Island and the coast of New Jersey there is something approaching to the sandy belt which has been left by the receding seas on the shores of Great Britain, but even there the long summer droughts leave the grass thin and wiry, so that the rolling turf of St Andrews is practically unknown. This great and essential obstacle has not, however, prevented the growth of the game in America. The national characteristics of energy and enterprise have, after a few years, solved the difficulty in no unsatisfactory manner. It is nearly ten years since the game was first thought of and played on this side of the Atlantic. But the real development of golf belongs to the last half-decade, and looking at it from that point of view the growth of the sport in America and the extraordinary ingenuity by which nearly every shortcoming has been conquered are most remarkable. The consequence is that a sort of golf has been developed here which is practically unknown either in England or Scotland.

In the older countries the player has to choose between a journey to the seaside

Golf in the USA. Top professionals Lloyd Mangrum, Ralph Guldahl, Craig Wood and Jimmy Demaret, assisted by actress Mary Woodfell (TV's first Lois Lane), do their bit for sales of US War Bonds. Hitler and Hirohito suffer.

and a very indifferent field for his favourite pursuit. With all the good will in the world, it is impossible to assert that there is any inland course, either in England or Scotland, which in any way approaches the links of Sandwich or St Andrews.

In America, on the other hand, courses have been built up in the last few years which, although inferior in a few respects to the genuine seaside courses, do afford not only an enjoyable game, but a real test of golfing ability.

This consummation has not been reached without a vast expense of money and a great deal of mental and physical labour. It was a long time before the real idea of the game could be instilled into the minds of those who had the charge of the various courses in the east of America. In nearly every case the holes were exactly the wrong distance apart, the hazards were badly placed, the putting greens were either extremely bad or far too small, and anything from a stone quarry to a pigeon trap was considered a legitimate feature of a good course.

It is not so long ago that a writer, of no mean ability as a penman, described in glowing terms the sporting qualities of links in which ploughed fields, railway tracks, and wooden pavilions added new elements of interest to the old Scotch game.

It is indeed extraordinary that with the large percentage of Scottish business

men throughout America there should not have been a wider-spread knowledge of the true requirements of a national pastime. It remained, however, for one or two men like Mr C. B. Macdonald, of the Chicago Golf Club, and Mr John Reed, of the St Andrews Club at Yonkers, to appeal again and again to the intelligence of American devotees in favour of courses laid out with some knowledge of what golf links ought to be. The efforts of a few men like these – combined with the growing impetus which has been given to the game by its universal popularity, both among older men and among college undergraduates – have at last succeeded in producing what is essentially a good American golf links.

A Sioux chief and his daughter in action at Sunningdale in 1910. They were there to promote Buffalo Bill's Wild West show.

H. J. Whigham, *Golf and Golfers*, 1899

PART THREE

GREAT CHAMPIONS, MEMORABLE CHAMPIONSHIPS

Introduction

The most visible face of golf is its top tournament professionals. Watched by millions worldwide, these masters of the sport regularly battle it out in major championships in front of vast television audiences. A missed putt, a hooked drive – the drama and emotion are there for everyone to see. But while the professional has been an integral part of the golf scene for almost two centuries, it is only over the last few decades that his status has risen from obscurity to pre-eminence. From humble caddy to modern-day golfing superstar, the 'rags to riches' rise of the golf professional has been nothing short of remarkable.

Modern-day golfing superstar Nick Faldo shows the drama and emotion when holing the winning putt in the 1989 World Match Play at Wentworth.

Going back to the dawn of professional golf in the mid-1800s, the first great champion eulogised for his golfing skill was four-time British Open winner, 'Old' Tom Morris Snr. Popular with everyone who knew him, he spent the years immediately before his death in 1906 greeting visiting golfers who would flock to his shop in St Andrews just to shake his hand and listen to his reminiscences. Despite being an educated man himself, 'Old' Tom was never inclined to write his own memoirs, and it is through the foresight of writers like Hutchinson and Tulloch that we have at least some idea of how the game was played in the early days of tournament golf.

Some years later, around the turn of the century, the professional game in Britain was dominated by three champions. Collectively known as the 'Great Triumvirate', Harry Vardon, James Braid and J. H. Taylor, won a remarkable sixteen British Open Championships between them in the two decades from 1894 to 1914. With competition fierce between the three men over such a long period, the golfing public thrilled at their exploits, while publishers fell over themselves to offer book contracts and endorsements. In later years, Vardon and Taylor took their talents to the United States playing a strenuous series of exhibition matches, as well as competing in the National Open Championship. As reports from golf writers of the period suggest, they, more than anyone else, contributed to the rapid growth of interest in America during the early 1900s.

Long before television, it is remarkable how these top professionals became as famous as they did. Today, tournament results from anywhere in the world are now instantly available, but less than half a century ago the British golfing public relied almost exclusively on newspaper and magazine reports for their information. In those seemingly far-off days, results arrived days, even weeks after the tournament had ended. Except for the occasional handful of grainy black and white photographs printed in a golf magazine, exotic-sounding venues like Shinnecock Hills and Pebble Beach were read about but rarely seen.

Yet, through the writing of journalists like Bernard Darwin for *The Times* and Harold Hilton for *Golf Monthly*, every amateur knew about the exploits of professionals like Vardon, Braid and Taylor. They could read about the drama and excitement caused by their close finishes in major championships, picturing it as if they were there themselves. Not only the professionals, but great women golfers like Joyce Wethered and Glenna Collett from the 1920s are also covered in this section. A nostalgic dip back into the game's glorious past, it reveals some of the drama and passion involved in world championship golf.

WILLIE PARK SNR – FIRST WINNER OF THE OPEN CHAMPIONSHIP IN 1860

In concluding this notice of Willie Park, Senr., although as a rule comparisons are odious, I should like to observe, regarding him and old Tom, that while Willie was the more brilliant player, Tom was the steadier. When Willie came out as a player, he was undoubtedly the first, but I should not like to say he was *facile princeps*, for in my opinion there never has been any golfer to whom this term could be applied. I do not think it admits of a shadow of a doubt that had Allan Robertson accepted Willie's challenge he would have had no better chance in the first few years of Willie's career than either Willie Dunn or Tom Morris.

The great features in Willie's play were his driving and his putting. His approach was scarcely so good, both old Tom and Willie's brother Davie being in my opinion better approachers with the iron. But as regards his driving and putting he was irreproachable. While many may have equalled him and possibly a few surpassed him in driving, no player in my opinion ever equalled him as a putter.

May his highly respected son hand down his reputation to posterity.

A. H. Doleman Letter to the Editor of *Golf* magazine, 1891

PLAYING IN THE ROAD

The seventeenth hole at St Andrews is the famous Road Hole, and the most historic in golf. It was on that hole that John Henry Taylor, needing only a six and a five, I think, to win the Open Championship, played over into the road and took thirteen strokes.

Watts Gunn and I collaborated at this same hole in one of the most terrifying bits of golf I have ever seen. It was in the Walker Cup matches in 1926 and we were playing Tolley and Jamieson in the Scotch foursomes, which means that each partner plays alternate strokes on the same ball.

Watts and Jamieson were driving. The drive here is supposed to go straight over the middle of a barn, which is out of bounds. Watts just got over, while Jamieson hit the building plumb in the middle, and Tolley had to play three off the tee. Cyril, made cautious by his partner's mistake, pulled his drive over in the first fairway.

It was now my turn and I played a conservative spoon shot short of, and in front of, the green. Jamieson topped the fourth for his team and Tolley, in an heroic effort to reach the green, went over into the road. That was five for our opponents and, being in the road, they would do well to go down in eight!

Watts and I looked certain to twin the hole. But nothing is ever certain on the seventeenth at St Andrews. Watts had to play a run-up to the very narrow green

Bobby Jones in the 1930 Gold Vase tournament at Sunningdale. It was a momentous year for him – and for golf – as he won the Grand Slam of all four Majors.

between the bunker on one side and the road on the other. He shanked into the road. Now, we were in the road in three, they in five.

Jamieson played a beautiful shot up twelve feet from the hole. That looked bad for us, for our ball was lying in the hard road. The hole was only fifteen or twenty feet away; the green was dry; and the terrible bunker was just beyond the flag. Watts and I put our heads together and indulged in a little mental arithmetic. We finally decided that if I should play down toward the brook behind the green, Watts could pitch back on so that two putts would give us a seven and a half, if Tolley holed his putt. We felt that we would be thankful for anything now.

We did get our seven. Tolley rimmed the long one, and we won the hole, but not until we had used up all our shots and most of the little brains we had.

Bobby Jones on Golf, 1930

BOBBY JONES

At the age of 28, Robert Tyre Jones, Jr., of Atlanta, Georgia – better known as Bobby Jones of all points North, East, South and West – stood upon the highest pinnacle of golfing fame, looking back on the most marvellous stretch of achievement ever reached by a golfer on either side of the Atlantic. There was nothing ahead left undone, no championship title that had escaped his attention; and anything that he might do in the years to come could only be an anticlimax to what he had just accomplished that summer. As far as he could see along the distant horizon from his lofty height nothing could be discerned but waste barren land that held no promise of a future.

With no more worlds to conquer the Atlanta barrister decided to put away his famous 'Calamity Jane' that had done such devastating work, along with the rest of his golfing weapons and call it a day.

In the spring of 1930 Bobby sailed for England, with seven other prominent young American amateurs, seeking another victory in the Walker Cup matches. Jones had other ideas in his mind that involved bigger game. For years he had been gunning for the British amateur championship but it had always managed to move out of range of his deadly fire each time. Those who had gathered at the dock to see the boys depart and wish them *bon voyage* – and a bit of luck on the other side – centred their hopes in Jones and expressed the wish that he might return with both British championships. Bobby's reply to his well wishers was that he would be quite satisfied with the amateur title and that there would be plenty of time to talk about the Open after he had successfully landed the first plum.

It is a matter of history that he had a close call in that first event, at the hands of an American and fellow teammate, George Voigt, but he managed to get away with it and that was all that mattered. Once snaring the elusive amateur title, he found it even less difficult to annex the Open and he set sail for home with both of these cherished possessions in his golfing kit.

Bobby's golfing dream was realised when he came back to American shores and completed his 'grand slam' by winning both the amateur and the Open titles, making a clean sweep of the four important major events in one year. This has all been too recent in golf history to warrant a detailed recital of what happened. All four of these championships, each one an achievement in itself and all the more remarkable when they came in a cluster, could not actually be counted the best golf that he had ever played. In analysing each event we find that not one of them showed exceptional golfing skill or outstanding play beyond the Jones standard, but they did show a tremendous amount of courage and fortitude and a display of nerve that has never been equalled. As he neared his goal the strain must have been intense. But the stout hearted young Georgian never faltered; he was bent solely on accomplishing his aim and determined to see it through.

Not Bobby Jones nor anyone else will ever again do as fine a thing in golf.

Bobby Jones, aged 14, during his first US Amateur Championship in 1916 at Merion Cricket Club. He beat one former champion before eventually being knocked out by the holder, Bob Gardner.

Realising full well that the records set down in this volume will last for generations to come, it is safe to predict that Jones' achievement will never be equalled. 'The impregnable quadrilateral of golf,' as George Trevor so aptly termed it, has been quite enough to place Jones on a lasting pedestal of fame; but Bobby, aside from this, occupied a pretty secure position in the world of golf in 1929. His record previous to the 'big event' will bear the closest scrutiny. Starting life as a boy wonder, Bob Jones was forced to take what came his way and make the best of it. Even as a youngster the impeccable Mr Jones of Georgia had many successes and many bitter disappointments which even to a boy didn't seem to be a square deal at the hands of Fate.

The earliest records of Bob Jones can be found in an old copy of *The American Golfer* printed in 1910, chronicling the deeds of a young lad by the name of Bobby Jones who at the age of eight had just won a golf tournament in Atlanta. Skipping over a few years we find this same young chap at the age of fourteen seeking national honours in the amateur championship at the Merion Cricket Club in Philadelphia in 1916. It is a strange coincidence that Bobby should have started his tournament career at Merion, won his first amateur title there and returned to play in his last national championship on these same links.

The youngster from Atlanta was a sensation at Merion in 1916 in more ways than one. His golf stood up for two rounds after the qualifying test but his golfing disposition came in for much criticism from the beginning. 'The kid wonder', as we golf writers called him, could play golf like a man and he could also swear like one when things went wrong. It was quite some time before he was able to master an uncontrollable desire to throw clubs at random and to use language unbecoming a gentleman, even allowing for liberties that the golf links are supposed to license. The golfing world had much time to speculate and wonder about the future of this precocious youngster in the next three years, since no major championships were played during the time we were engaged in the World War.

Bobby filled in his time playing in Red Cross matches and improving his game. He attracted attention wherever he appeared and his performance was highly satisfactory. He was a match for anyone, amateur or pro. Long Jim Barnes stopped off at Atlanta one day and played in an exhibition against Bobby in which the latter astonished Jim by his ability to throw clubs and otherwise disport himself like a spoiled child. Jim, in telling about his experience with the boy a few weeks later, remarked that there was nothing wrong with Bobby's disposition. 'Any golfer,' said Jim, 'who is as determined to play topnotch golf and win matches as he is will make a champion some day. Mark my words, the kid is there and we are going to hear a lot about him in the next few years.'

Bobby turned out to be a terrible disappointment to those who had figured that his golfing temperament would ruin him, and had thought that if he ever did succeed in winning there would be no living with him. In 1919 when he was runner-up to Dave Herron at Oakmont there was a complete change. Here was a modest little chap taking his beating in the final in a championship that he would have loved to win, and not grumbling about it. In the next few years he had learned to take it on the chin, even though he didn't exactly relish the idea of not being able to win one of the big major events. But he was becoming dissatisfied with his lot.

There was a time when Jones seriously considered giving up the game, and had it not been for his victory in the Open at Inwood in 1923 he would have been lost to golf. His greatest disappointment came in 1922 at Brookline. He was the outstanding favourite to win this amateur championship, and when he was turned back by Jess Sweetser in the semi-finals by the highly decisive margin of 7 up and 6 to play it was a bitter pill to swallow. O. B. Keeler, who always had Bobby's confidence, remarked at the time that it looked like the beginning of the end for the Atlanta youngster.

'Bobby has had several shots at the amateur championship,' said Keeler, 'and if the old dame who guides the destinies of golf champions is going to treat him like it did here he will be among the missing next year. Bobby has ambitious plans for a business career, and these plans do not include any golf. I wouldn't be surprised but what you have seen the last of us in golf championships. When Bobby quits I will quit too.'

There were times when Jones had to take the bitter with the sweet and profess to like it. As we look back on these upsets now they appear of minor importance. One disturbance was the distressing defeat at the hands of Walter Hagen in Florida in '26 by the rather humiliating score of 12 and 11. It was just Walter's time to shine, and there was nothing Bobby could do about it. Another occasion that was none too pleasant was when, under the sunny skies of California in 1929, he was stopped in the first round of the amateur championship at Pebble Beach by Johnnie Goodman. Bobby's admirers and well wishers were really more disturbed over this than he was, as he admitted he had never really seen an amateur championship before from a spectator's standpoint.

There is always one achievement that stands out in a champion's mind as his own pet stellar achievement. Bobby knows which tournament he got the greatest kick out of winning. It was the Open at Sciote where he scrambled under the wire a stroke ahead of Joe Turnesa. It was a great victory because he was forced to do something worthwhile to win it. With nine holes to play it was seen that Jones could beat the score just turned in by Turnesa if he could manage the rest of the journey home in par figures. His march home that day was something long to be remembered, so seldom does the winner come to the home hole in a blaze of glory. Usually the stretch-running is where the hopes of many golfers are dashed to the rocks. Instead of being able to deliver their best, the players find a signal to fold up and become lost in the general scramble.

Jones didn't falter for a single instant that afternoon. Once he had his work laid out for him he went about the task like a master workman, and when he had finished there was just that one stroke that told the story. In the locker room that

afternoon the pros held an indignation meeting, each blaming the other for letting Bobby come through. Hagen told the boys what he thought about it and he didn't mince words. 'Every time I happen to be going badly,' said Walter, 'all the rest of you quit on the job. If we don't stop this lad he will be walking away with all our championships. Amateurs have won our Open five times now, out of the last twelve tournaments, and that is just a few times too many.'

There is hardly any question but what Jones had become a threatening menace to the pros. He was an additional hazard in every championship and one that wrecked the scores of many players with chances for victory in sight. Hardly a pro could be said to be scot-free of the Bobby Jones complex. Some pros admitted it openly, others stumbled into the pit unconsciously; but one thing is certain, at one time or another they all fell, and it was not an easy task to scramble to their feet. Usually during the progress of a tournament the cry from one end of the links to the other was 'How is Jones going?' Most of the players were so busy worrying about the entry from Atlanta that they had no time to concentrate on their own games. This made Jones' task doubly easy and often paved his way to victory when it might have been otherwise.

It was charged that the governing body had something to do with making Bobby's life a happy one on the links. The pros were whispering around that Jones was getting all the breaks. He could pick his own partner and had the choice of the starting time. If there were special rules to be interpreted a bevy of friendly officials were on hand to perform this function. Always he carried a bodyguard of

Bobby Jones holing his second shot on the par-4 fourth in the 1930 British Amateur Championship at St Andrews. He went on to take the title – the first on his way to the Grand Slam.

officials on and off the links. This was beginning to be a sore spot with the entire professional brigade and it meant an additional worry.

The U.S.G.A. may have favoured Jones, consciously or unconsciously, but usually there was some good reason. The increased galleries when the Atlanta barrister was at his height is explanation enough to clear up the mystery. Jones was drawing the crowds and the people's interest had to be looked after. It was a one-man show for a while and it was a profitable performance. Naturally the star is entitled to the best dressing room and the breaks of attention up and down the line. If any of the other actors didn't like it all they had to do was to step in and steal the show. It was not so easy to do as a rule, but sometimes it happened.

Bobby Jones' career was all too short to allow any correct opinion of what he might have done in later years. That he was truly a very great artist there can be no doubt, and whatever he has done he has left an indelible impression upon the minds of golfers who knew him during his tournament days. To be compelled to write about one so young in the past tense is difficult, for there is always the possibility that he may burst out at any time and start a new career. This seems unlikely when one knows the former youthful prodigy as well as the author – but stranger things than that have happened in golf.

H. B. Martin, *50 Years of American Golf*, 1936

GRAND NATIONAL GOLF-CLUB TOURNAMENT

Edinburgh, 10th June 1857
The Committee appointed to take the management of the details of a Grand National Golf Club Tournament, met this day, and agreed to the following resolutions:–

1*st*, That the Tournament shall take place at St Andrews on Wednesday the 29th July, and following days. Play to commence each day at Twelve o'clock.

2*d*, All Golf Clubs shall have the right of competing, on payment of £4; and notice of their intention to enter the lists must be sent to the Convener of the Committee on or before the 10th July. The Subscriptions to be paid at the same time.

3*d*, The Prize shall be a handsome piece of Silver Plate with Golfing Device.

4*th*, Each competing Club shall elect two Representative Members, who shall play throughout as partners, and whose names must be posted in the Union Club-House, St Andrews, by Four o'clock on the evening of the 28th July; after which no change can be made.

5*th*, Opponents shall be drawn by lot before each start, Club against Club.

6*th*, The winners of the first set of Matches shall be drawn in the same manner for the second set, and so on till one winning couple is left. In the event of an odd number of competing couples for any of the sets, the odd couple, as drawn by lot, shall play in the following set.

7*th*, The Club represented by the winning couple shall be considered the Champion Club till the next Tournament, and be entitled to the prize.

8*th*, The Matches shall be the best of thirty holes, being one round of the links and six holes out and home. If any Matches are halved, both couples shall be drawn again in the next set; and if the final set is halved, a Match of eighteen holes shall be played till the prize is won.

9*th*, An Umpire to be appointed by the majority of the competing Clubs present, whose decision in all cases shall be final. He shall be guided by the rules of St Andrew's Golf-Club, and may take advice if he chooses.

J. WHYTE MELVILLE, *Convener.*

J. O. FAIRLIE.

O. G. CAMPBELL.

R. HAY.

P.S. – *All communications must be addressed to the Convener,*
J. Whyte Melville, Esq., *Mount Melville, St Andrews.*

THE MAKING OF THE MASTERS

The United States Masters tournament is all about tradition. Held each spring at the exclusive Augusta National Golf Club in Georgia, it remains a privately run event for a small, select number of golf professionals. In keeping with the high ideals of the club's founder Bobby Jones, it has an enviable reputation for quality and efficiency. The only one of golf's four majors played at the same venue each year, the beauty of Augusta's azalea-lined fairways has captivated golfers world-wide for over sixty years. Born decades after the two big Opens – the British and American – the Masters has risen to challenge these older, more established fixtures as the most prestigious test in golf.

Apart from being the original inspiration for the Masters tournament, Bobby Jones was also the driving force behind the Augusta National Golf Club. After competing his legendary Grand Slam of 1930, he shocked the golfing world by announcing his retirement from big-time competition. Though still only 28, Jones had no intention of giving up the game that had been his life. Content to stay out of the tournament spotlight, he concentrated his efforts on a wider range of golfing projects. He joined A. G. Spalding, helping to design the next generation of golf equipment. He also filmed a series of instructional movie shorts for Warner Bros as well as broadcasting his own radio show. Bobby Jones was now slowly achieving all his ambitions, but he still had one particular project in mind.

While visiting the small Georgia town of Augusta late in 1930, Jones had met with New York banker, Clifford Roberts, who often vacationed there. Sharing a natural love of golf they became close friends. Discussing the great courses they had both played, Jones confided his longheld desire to build the perfect golf course. Situated somewhere in the heart of the South, the 'dream' course would incorporate some of the great holes that he had played on during his tournament career. Roberts became keenly interested in the idea, suggesting a particular piece of land just west of Augusta that might be suitable. Intrigued by Clifford Roberts's description, they went to look at the site shortly after on a cold, December morning. Bobby Jones took one look and knew it would be perfect.

Originally an old indigo plantation known as Fruitlands, a Belgian nobleman had bought the land in 1857 and turned it into a nursery. He had planted magnolia seeds along the drive that led to his mansion and let his horticultural flair run wild over the rest of the 365-acre site. Apart from establishing a forest of stately pines, he had introduced a veritable garden wonderland of camellia, azalea and dogwood. Jones later remarked: 'Frankly, I was overwhelmed by the exciting possibilities of a golf course set in the midst of such a nursery.'

The decision made, Jones and Roberts set about turning their dream into a reality. With property prices hit by the Depression, they bought the land at a good price. Canvassing rich friends, a holding company was set up and plans mapped out for the formation of a private club. Membership was by invitation only, with a maximum of 30 coming from the Augusta area. The joining fee was put at $350, with the annual fee set at $60.

With the Augusta National Golf Club now reality, the respected Scottish golf architect, Alister MacKenzie, was invited to join Bobby Jones in laying out the actual course. Having spent many hours walking over his imaginary golf holes, Jones already had a clear idea of what he wanted. In his initial discussions with MacKenzie, Jones was adamant that as much as possible of the original nursery should be retained, including trees, shrubs and flowers. He maintained that it should be as scenic as possible. Strongly in favour of penalising the golfer around the greens rather than off the tee, his idea was to have broad, uncluttered fairways which gave the thoughtful golfer several lines of attack. Jones also disliked prohibitively long par-fives and pressed for shorter, more strategic holes where accuracy rather than brute strength was rewarded.

Work began in the spring of 1931 and finished eighteen months later in the autumn of 1932. Alister MacKenzie later described Augusta National as 'my finest achievement'. In a design that was considered revolutionary in the 1930s, the course had wide fairways, massive undulating greens and less than 22 bunkers at a time when most championship venues had over 200. Sadly, MacKenzie died shortly after the club was established and never had the opportunity to see his great course put to the test. A white, colonial-style mansion was built as the clubhouse, with a tree-lined driveway leading up to the front entrance, while a rear balcony overlooked the ninth and eighteenth greens. Ed Dudley was appointed the first professional and Augusta National Golf Club was born.

Designed purely as a private members' course, there was never any intention of using it for professional tournaments. Jones himself had always wanted it to be a place where friends got together to play golf in beautiful surroundings, but the fame of Augusta began to spread far beyond the Southern heartlands.

By the early 1930s, interest in golf had declined. Bobby Jones's sudden retirement from the game had left a void which not even the charismatic Gene Sarazen could fill. The American public who had taken golf to their hearts in 1930, associated the game entirely with Jones, and in their minds, without Jones there was no game. The first professional tour was struggling to make any impression, with only a limited number able to make a living from it. Golf desperately needed a boost. It desperately needed a professional tournament in the South, in 'Bobby Jones country'.

The first person to raise the subject was textile tycoon Fielding Wallace. As well as being active in the US Golf Association, later serving as President, Wallace was also a charter member of Augusta National. In late 1932, he proposed that the US Open should be held at Augusta, and presented his idea to the membership for approval. It was rejected unanimously, but then came the suggestion that perhaps

The final hole at the Augusta National. Competitors must face this intimidating corridor of trees if they are to win the Masters.

the club itself could put on its own tournament. After much debate, it was finally agreed and plans were quickly put in motion for Augusta's first professional event.

A strictly invitation only-event, the field would be drawn from the greatest players in the game. It would include all past winners of the United States Amateur and Open titles still living, plus the leading 24 players from the previous year's US Open at North Shore. The tournament would be played on the final weekend in March 1934, over 72 holes of medal play, one round each for four days. The prize fund of $5,000 would be supplied by the Augusta members and the tournament would be called the Augusta National invitation. Cliff Roberts had suggested the title 'Masters', but Bobby Jones vetoed the idea on the grounds that it sounded too pompous.

Roberts had also insisted that Jones should play in his own event to help guarantee its popularity. Jones flatly refused, stating that he had determined never to play competitive golf again after 1930. 'I then pointed out to him,' said Roberts many years later, 'that as host, he couldn't very well invite his golfing friends to come and play his course and then not play himself.' Jones finally relented, agreeing to play at least until the tournament had established itself.

At 10.00 am on Thursday, 22 March the legendary Robert T. Jones Jnr stepped on to the first tee at Augusta. The gallery numbered over one thousand, and they all followed Jones. Since the news broke about his tournament comeback, the American newspapers and public had talked of little else. High excitement swept the golfing world, and for the first time in four long years, golf was front-page news. Still aged only 32, Bobby Jones had played well in practice, scoring a 65, but the day before the first round, things began to go wrong; although he used a replica of the famed 'Calamity Jane' putter he had donated to the Royal and Ancient Golf Club Museum, he struggled desperately to find his putting touch. Playing erratically in the pro-amateur event, Jones went into the tournament lacking any degree of confidence whatsoever.

Unsteady with his short game, lacking the radar accuracy of his iron shots of only four years before and partnering a youthful Paul Runyan, Jones three-putted three of the last five greens to finish with an opening score of 76 – 4 over par. The second round saw little improvement. Playing into a freezing wind all day, Jones ended with a 74, including one missed putt from ten inches. With a 36-hole total of 150, the legendary Grand Slammer was eight shots behind halfway leader Horton Smith. Despite putting better for a third round 72, Jones now found himself ten shots behind the gentle giant Smith.

The final day was filled with nostalgia, as Jones was partnered with the great Walter Hagen for the last round. Hagen, now 42, was coming to the end of his own playing career, and after having been in contention after the opening day, had fallen back badly. Bobby Jones had 72, while Hagen rocketed to 77. The tournament itself had a close finish with five players battling it out down the final stretch including the 'home-pro' Ed Dudley. Eventually, the halfway leader Horton

Smith finally triumphed by a single stroke with his score of 70-70-70-74 for a winning total of 284.

Four years in the making, Augusta National Golf Club and its invitational tournament were declared resounding successes by players and press alike. In the second year its reputation for producing spectacular finishes was further enhanced by Gene Sarazen's famed double eagle on the fifteenth hole in the final round. Going on to beat Craig Wood in the first 36-hole play-off, Sarazen put his name on the rollcall of Masters winners that now reads like a 'Who's Who' of golfing greats.

Sadly, Bobby Jones, to whom Augusta owes everything, died in December 1971 of a crippling spinal disease. While his individual place in golf history is assured, the permanent legacy of the Augusta National and the Masters tournament played over it each spring, will leave golf in his debt forever.

Dale Concannon, *Golf: The Early Days*, 1995

CORRECT FORM

My dear Mr Hart,

The Silver Trophy in connection with the Open Championship Golf meeting, which was held on your green this year, and won by Mr John Ball Jnr, arrived safely this morning and is now in my custody until it is further wanted next year – I presume at St Andrews.

I notice that the inscription 'John Ball Jnr' is put on. 'John Ball Jnr?' Like the others I think this is a mistake and should read 'Mr John Ball Jnr'. As it is, it could be easily remedied by engraving the word in brackets *amateur* underneath. I can have this done in Liverpool and wait your reply to know what I am to do.

I presume this is sufficient acknowledgment of the Cup or Trophy.

Signed and dated 18th Oct. 1890.
Thomas Owen Potter (Secretary of Royal Liverpool Golf Club)

Letter to the secretary of Prestwick Golf Club commenting on the inscription on the British Open trophy. As in cricket, there was a clear distinction between gentleman amateurs and professionals during this period. The word 'amateur' was subsequently added next to his name.

THE DREAM BEGINS

In 1934 a young man named Henry Cotton stood on the 18th green at the Royal St George's Golf Club, Sandwich, in Kent, acknowledging the cheers of the joyous spectators. He had just won the Open Golf Championship and had brought the trophy and title back home again after a ten-year run of American triumphs.

Proudly watching his success were two golfing figures of the past, J. H. Taylor and James Braid, two members of the 'Great Triumvirate'. The third member, ill and barely able to walk, had sat near to the 6th green during the previous rounds watching the competitors pass by, but his strength gave out on the final day and he was confined to bed in a local hotel.

Directly after being handed the coveted trophy, Cotton hastened around to the nearby Guildford Hotel and placed the silver claret jug in the arms of the legendary Harry Vardon. Tears ran down the face of Vardon as he congratulated Cotton and clasped the cup in his arms, the famous trophy that he must have regarded as his own personal property: the trophy that acclaims his name six times over, a record that has remained unequalled since he captured the title on the last occasion in 1914.

In 1933 Vardon had been quoted as saying – 'Henry Cotton has proved his capability and I have high hopes of his future.' Cotton did indeed justify those views held by a man who was then a legend in his own lifetime. The name of Harry Vardon is synonymous with golf and it is difficult to pick up a book on the subject without his name appearing somewhere among the pages. Some fifty years after his death his name is still capable of steering conversation back through the mists of time and his influence on the game which he loved so dearly lives on.

Comparisons between sporting champions from different playing eras are pointless for each champion has his or her own special talent, setting standards which inspire others to rise to the heights of their own individual skills; but once in a while a genius comes along and, without doubt, Vardon is one of the greatest golfers ever to step forward on to a golf course.

When he died in 1937 he left behind a legacy of style, expertise and skill which thousands have tried to emulate over the years, some more successful in their aspirations than others. His achievements are all the more to be admired as he was dogged by ill-health at the peak of his career and he had to battle with lost strength to attain success when others might well have given in to the limitations of stamina.

'The Vardon Grip', internationally known and copied, was made universally popular by the charismatic Vardon – for charismatic he was with an elegant style and a professional approach to golf which were like a breath of fresh air after the slightly more primitive hitting techniques of his predecessors and contemporaries, and which earned him the title of 'The Stylist'.

He was also to have another nickname given to him by his peers, that of 'The Greyhound', supposedly first thought of by Andrew Kirkaldy, a fellow professional from Scotland, who, having witnessed Vardon overtaking him on so many

Harry Vardon, pictured early in his career, displays his famous grip. His rival Andrew Kirkaldy nicknamed him 'The Greyhound' because of his late surges in competitions.

occasions to win tournaments, was heard to mutter to bystanders – 'Watch the greyhound, watch the greyhound.'

Kirkaldy, an outstanding player of his generation, was never able to beat Vardon, although he had many victories over J. H. Taylor, James Braid, and Sandy Herd, another top Scottish player. Kirkaldy once said – 'If twenty of the best professionals were asked to write down the names of the four greatest golfers, they would put down Vardon, Taylor, Braid and Herd. If these four were asked to name the greatest among them, all save Vardon would put a cross against his name.'

In his book published in 1943, J. H. Taylor, a great rival, stated – 'My solemn and considered judgement is that Harry Vardon is the finest and most finished golfer the game has ever produced. This judgement I give after watching every player over some fifty years... he was a natural golfer. His beautiful and graceful style was the result of his inherent genius for the game.'

Vardon never had a golfing lesson; his was a pure natural talent which he gradually improved by watching others in his early days and incorporating and adapting those techniques best suited to his own style of play. He was first in hitting the ball higher into the air as, during practice, he realised that by so doing he could place the ball with greater accuracy. He developed his own near and upright stance which was quite innovative compared to the playing style of other golfers of the day. The Scottish patriarchs of the game, particularly those from St Andrews, had traditionally adopted a wide stance, lashing out at the ball with a mighty strength to counteract the strong winds blowing in from the North Sea.

Vardon's action was much more attractive to watch. The temperate climate of Jersey had allowed him to experiment with softer and more elegant strokes and his early years of observation, endless practice and technical skill resulted in a unique golfing style. He had the perfect figure for an athlete, slim with not an ounce of surplus fat, supple as a cane and his large hands were able to show off the overlapping grip to perfection.

Born with a rare gift of being in complete control of his emotions when playing golf, his ability to use every club with immaculate skill made those who were privileged to see him play envious of his talent. He was blessed with a wonderful concentration, so much so that Kirkaldy believed that 'even a gunshot ten feet away would not put him off his stroke'.

J. H. Taylor looked upon him as a golf artist. 'Vardon also had tolerance, understanding and a great modesty which belied the fact that he was the greatest golfer.'

Vardon did indeed remain exceedingly modest throughout his life over his considerable achievements and his status in the world of golf. He had been grateful for the talent that fate had bestowed upon him, but always remained a little surprised at the amount of world-wide attention he had commanded.

In the early 1930s one of his neighbours happened to see some old newsreel at the local cinema showing Vardon playing at the height of his fame, and the next day he remarked over the garden fence to Vardon's wife – 'I know Mr Vardon is a champion gardener; I didn't know he was a champion golfer.'

With all his popularity and worldly travels, he never became big-headed or filled with his own importance. He was keen to talk about golfing techniques but did not draw particular attention to his own accomplishments. After an interview with him, one newspaper reporter wrote – 'While positive on his golf views, Vardon is not a great talker nor is he at all of a boastful nature.'

The brassie, niblick, mashie and cleek were his clubs, the gutta-percha his ball, and with these at his disposal he created magical happenings on the fairways and greens of Great Britain, Europe and North America. He was so consistently

*Six times British
Open champion,
Harry Vardon.*

accurate with his shots that, given an indicated spot, he could hit the ball time after time to that precise target.

During a tour of the United States in 1900, his first visit to that country, the American professionals used to tell their young compatriots – 'He doesn't like to play a course twice in the same day. Why not? Well, he's so accurate with his shots that during the second round his ball finishes up in the very divot holes he made that morning and so it takes all the fun out of the game for him.'

This was a charming, humorous story but factually incorrect. Those who witnessed Vardon's skill on the fairways usually remarked on how cleanly he hit the ball, hardly disturbing a blade of grass with his iron shots.

It was the consistency of his play that so enthralled the American public and they thronged the fairways to see 'the great Harry Vardon' in action. An unknown American wrote of him – 'He proves as no man does that golf is an art. It is pure joy to him and for those who watch. He makes every shot look effortless.'

However, the tour of the United States and his seduction of the American golfing community were a dream far distant from his humble beginnings. He did not seek golf, golf found him and it is extremely doubtful whether he would have embarked on a sporting profession without the hand of fate bringing the game to his island home. He would possibly have remained involved in gardening, living a quiet existence with neither the thoughts nor the means to travel the world. As he himself remarked – 'If they had failed to bring golf to Jersey, I might still have been spending my life in horticultural pursuits.'

As it was, he was surrounded by the world of golf at an early age and he played, in the beginning, through curiosity, discovering during his formative years that he had an aptitude for a game which at that time only served as a pleasurable pastime. It was to be many years before he realised that he could actually turn a hobby into the means of earning a living.

His brother, Tom, also proficient in the game, was instrumental in encouraging Vardon to pursue a career in golf and it was this sibling support which helped him on his way to success. 'I owe so much – everything – to the great game of golf,' Vardon said at the end of his career, and this was certainly true, knowing the path his life had taken. The scenario was one of which dreams are made but seldom fulfilled.

Vardon, however, was one of the fortunate few, his incredible mastery of the game opening up a new and exciting world. He capitalised on his natural talent with hard work, dedication and an iron will to succeed.

For one who achieved such stature in his chosen career, he did not readily enforce his theories and techniques on to others, rather the reverse, as he followed the maxim 'actions speak louder than words', preferring to demonstrate his skill out on the golf course – a master class for all who cared to watch.

A quiet man, pleasantly humoured, Vardon greatly enjoyed the comradeship of his fellow golfers but at the same time remained an intensely private individual. He was a lonely man, in a sense, for once away from the golf course and his colleagues, he found no outlet for his emotional needs at home. His wife, Jessie, was not interested in golf and therefore unable to understand and share with him the inevitable joys and disappointments attached to such a competitive sport. She would have preferred a less public face for her husband and, in all probability, would have been far more contented had he remained a gardener, an anonymous occupation which she would have found easier to accept than the vocation of a professional golfer.

Vardon's strength of character was fully tested by the traumas attached to his childless marriage and he had to cope with the pain of bereavement while still struggling to make his mark on the golfing world. However, at an age when most have come to terms with the familiar pattern of their private lives, he met a young lady and formed a romantic attachment. Of necessity, it was a secret relationship but it filled a gap in his life and brought him happiness when he most needed it. The liaison resulted in the birth of a child, but here too Vardon was denied lasting joy and in the fullness of time the episode was to bring its own particular sorrow.

Throughout all his tribulations, Vardon immersed himself in his golf, finding it a comforting salvation. 'Golf has no equal as a test of human strengths and failings,' he said, a test which he faced many times and which he passed with flying colours. To his brother professionals, and indeed all those who came into contact with him, Vardon was a 'gentleman', both on and off the course.

For his part, Vardon expressed his feelings towards his colleagues thus – 'The fact that I should have been fortunate enough to spend so many years in close association with such a splendid type of sportsman is one of the happiest memories of my golfing life.'

Audrey Howell, *Harry Vardon – The Revealing Story of a Champion Golfer*, 1991

NOT AS IT WAS

The time was when a mistake at any place was severely punished; now the Course can be 'skuttered' without much loss. Then the Course was narrow, the bunkers were yawning traps for topped balls, the whins were deadly snares for screwed or heeled gutties; now one can slip along the side without risking anything. I remember old George Glennie looking sadly at the filling-up 'Tam's Coo' bunker as a Knight of old would regard the dead body of an honoured and valiant rival; and he was the best golfer of his day. Where now is the nervous danger of crossing 'hell' on to the Elysian Fields? Where the sure punishment of the 'Beardies' for a missed stroke? Both are left as historical terrors; no one now requires to risk them.

The putting greens too are quite changed. Then there was a variety of surface which brought out the greatest skill; now all are nicely turfed over and artificially dressed like billiard tables. Then at the 'Heather-hole' one had to dodge about and watch the lie of the green, carefully noting any hollow to catch or 'soo-back' to avoid in the gentle stroke; thereby, as old Robbie Paterson used to say 'wilin' the wether into the hoose'. Now no caddy's advice is needed, no look is required from the hole end to 'study' the ground; a dead, straight putt suffices. The 'Sandy-hole' puzzled the uninitiated with its heavy putting surface; now it is a stroke easier. The 'Corner of the Dyke' was most precarious; now it is easily approached. The 'Home-hole' had its treacherous undulations to tax the ability of the player; now it is all a dead plateau. Such changes have broken the score-chain – six strokes on the round are at least saved. Allan Robertson's 79 is not now understood or properly appreciated.

Rev J. G. McPherson, *Golf and Golfers Past and Present*, 1891

TOM MORRIS v WILLIE PARK

Both players then retired for refreshments. In a short time Park appeared on the teeing-ground; but the St Andrews champion not putting in an appearance, the excitement amongst the crowd became great. It was shortly ascertained that the referee had decided that play in the remaining 6 holes of the match should be postponed till Saturday forenoon at eleven o'clock. Park protested against this, the more especially as he had not been consulted, and stated that if Morris did not come forward and finish the round, he would do so by himself and claim the stakes. Morris abided by the decision of the referee who stated that his reason for postponing the play was 'That notwithstanding all exertions no means were practicable for keeping back the onlookers, some of whom by their conduct rendered the play an impossibility'. Park by himself, followed by the large crowd, played the remaining holes. This he did in fine style. His score for the last 6 holes was 4, 4, 3, 4, 5 and 2=22. On Saturday morning at eleven o'clock, the hour appointed by Mr Robert Chambers for playing off the 6 holes left unplayed, Morris and a few spectators appeared at the end hole. Park was present but he adhered to the view he had taken of the referee's duties, maintaining that he had played out the match on the day fixed by the articles, viz. the 22nd April. That no man had any power to stop the play in the middle of the game. That, as Morris had refused to play out the last 6 holes when called on by him, he had done so by himself, and therefore won the match. He accordingly refused to play the 6 holes with Morris on Saturday morning unless a new match were made. Mr Chambers directed Morris to walk the course, which he did, holing the 6 holes from Mr Forman's in 4, 4, 5, 5, 6 and 4 respectively – 28 in all. At the conclusion Morris was loudly hissed by the partisans of the Musselburgh champion, as was the referee, who gave the following written decision in the course of the forenoon: – 'As referee in the match between Morris and Park on April 22nd and in terms of my decision, the remaining 6 holes were played by Morris this day, Park declining to finish the game. I therefore declare Morris to be the winner. (Signed) R. Chambers, jun., Musselburgh, April 23rd, 1870.'

Of these (the leaders before named) Mr Ball led the way, and although off the tee and through the green he showed no falling off, he was frequently short in his long putts, and with a 79 his aggregate was 308, thus furnishing a cue to the others as to what they had to beat. Hugh Kirkaldy preserved his good form of the forenoon, and driving to the last hole had a five to beat Mr Ball; but he pitched into the ditch guarding the green with his third, and, although he made a grand recovery, it took him six, and so he dead-heated with the amateur Champion. Herd a couple or two behind, had also a similar figure to head the poll, but he missed an easy putt and was consequently bracketed level with the other two. From the rear, however, came such glowing accounts of Mr Hilton's progress, that nearly everyone rushed to where he and his partner, Jack Ferguson, then were, and with an enthusiastic and ever increasing following they made their way home. At the turn Mr Hilton had drawn level with Mr Ball, and forging steadily ahead on the home coming, he had twenty to tie with four holes to go. A three and a five to the next two gave him eleven to win driving to the second last green. Here Jack Ferguson created a sensation by getting down in two, but when Mr Hilton's ball found the bottom in one more, all was over, bar accidents. A six to the home hole completed a grand round, played with the greatest confidence and dash, and, amidst general cheering, Mr Hilton was hailed as Champion for the year. With a fine free style, he is one of the most rapid players we have ever seen, taking little or no time to judge his shots; and his partner, Jack Ferguson, who likes plenty of time, seemed thoroughly glad when the round was over.

The Golfing Annual, 1892-93

A PROFESSIONAL FOUL

A brilliant amateur was one day playing a rather tricky professional at St Andrews. A fair gallery was in attendance to see the splendid play. The game had been going on very steadily, most of the holes having been halved; and at the Corner-of-the-Dyke hole the match was all square and two to play. Both drove well off the tee, and they had to approach the hole at the Swilken Burn... The Burn was in flood. The amateur was in doubt as to what club he should take, and thought of his cleek. Suddenly the professional turned to his caddy and said pretty loudly, 'See ma lang spune, laddie!' His unsuspicious antagonist changed his mind and took his long spoon and drove right into the Burn. Then the wily fellow, who had made his loud remark for this very purpose, smiled grimly, took his cleek, and lay on the green, winning the hole, putting his opponent out of temper, and gaining the match.

Rev J. G. McPherson, *Golf and Golfers Past and Present*, 1891

TRICKS OF THE TRADE

If we consider the plausible and insidious means by which these tricks insinuate themselves into a golfer's affections, it is not so much to be wondered at that he is conquered. By their aid he finds himself suddenly steady, able to beat adversaries previously dreaded, and to win handicap electro-plate with strokes to spare. At first they do not even shorten driving, the diseases taking some time to get into the system and cripple the other members. By the time they have done so it is too late to get rid of them. The player works through stages of foozling and, after as long a period as it would have taken to be a pretty golfer, he comes out a robust cripple, ungainly although perhaps strong. This is the prognosis in the most favourable cases, but some would-be golfers are restless in the use of remedies. They employ device after device, add fault to fault. No sooner is their driving weakened by assimilating one, than another and yet another, infallibly 'steadier' presents itself, and is accepted, till at last there is not a chance of their cleanest-hit ball going more than fifty yards. They call themselves the steady players. Steady indeed! They top and puff quite as often, if not oftener, than those who have acquired their game with less prejudice. They are steady only because it does not matter to their

The dreaded foozle.

partners whether they hit or miss, and straight, because wildness is not appreciable in very short distances. Any morning we can see men out aiming at a style instead of at a ball. A trial swing now and then, especially before starting, may do no harm. There are even good players who indulge a good deal in this amusement. These one can distinguish from the deluded creatures who are teaching themselves styles by the free, thoughtless way in which they let out. The others – earnest, careful, apparently concentrated on the blade of grass in front of them – do not hear 'Fore – stop that – hurry up' shouted behind them; for their mind is busy committing to memory their last patent gyration. If the fools would but reflect on a certain passage of Scripture they might learn that neither leopard nor golf spotting can be managed by taking thought, and that thought will not add cubits either to their stature or to their driving. From the latter it will take some off.

Sir Walter Simpson, The Art of Golf, 1887

F. G. TAIT – THE PERFECT AMATEUR

Apart from the beauty of his manner of hitting the ball there was something very pleasant to watch about the light-hearted, confident, yet reserved way in which he acted when he engaged in a match. A good golfing temperament is as important as a good golfing style, and Tait was blessed beyond most men in this respect. If the true golfing temperament be fitly described as a blending of the qualities of the general and the philosopher, Tait possessed the ideal disposition to perfection. He played the game with his head all the time, and when misfortune overtook him, his philosophical turn of mind enabled him to make the most of the possibilities of the case.

If the gallery loved Tait, Tait also delighted in the gallery, and was always seen at his best when playing with a large following. Fear, conceit and self-consciousness are the three things which make a man 'funk' before a crowd. It wounds the pride of a man to play badly when people are watching him, and in striving to play too well he does not play his natural game and fails. The moment a player begins to speculate as to what the spectators are thinking of him, he loses the power of concentrating his attention upon his stroke, which is essential to the proper striking of the ball. The conceited young player may make a good start, before a crowd, but he will get a rude awakening before the match is over; the modest man will gain confidence as the round proceeds.

Tait's nature knew nothing of fear, pride or self-consciousness and for that reason he always played his best when others less gifted would have lost their heads. 'Modest' is an epithet which has been applied to Tait's manner in playing so often and by so many writers, that it must undoubtedly express a very popular impression. But I do not think that 'modest' is a term which really *fully* expresses his conduct when golfing, for there was plenty of light-hearted confidence about his style, and he never went out to play a match with the appearance of one who thought there was any likelihood of defeat. His manner strikes me as being better expressed by the word 'natural'. Everything he did was done without any striving after effect; he took his successes as if he expected them and his bad luck as part of the chances of the game.

John L. Low, *F. G. Tait, A Record,* 1900

THE PRESTWICK LINKS

As a centre of Golf, Ayrshire occupies in the West of Scotland the position that Fifeshire does in the East. It is now, and is likely to remain, the chief seat of Golf in the West, and it contains more Golf links and more golf clubs than all that remains of the West of Scotland placed together. And what St Andrews is to Fifeshire and the East, Prestwick is to Ayrshire and the West, the richest in incident and the most important in the recent annals of Golf. In respect of historical records within the last thirty years Prestwick with its premier club occupies a place not second even to St Andrews and the Royal and Ancient. As compared with the antiquity of the Royal and Ancient it is, of course, a comparatively modern institution, but during three of the four decades of its existence it has kept pace with its elder and larger rival in maintaining, promoting, and encouraging the game of Golf. St Andrews is the Mecca of the golfer, but Prestwick is the Medina, and no enthusiast would consider his pilgrimage complete who had not visited the last named place as well as the former.

It is invidious to make comparison sometimes, and I am not anxious to set off Prestwick against St Andrews, especially to the disadvantage of the latter. But everything in this objective world is comparative, and one must have some approximate equivalent to set one's comparisons against. There is one circumstance that gives Prestwick the advantage over St Andrews, the circumstance that a considerable portion of the links is the property of the club. Lord Wellwood has aptly written that 'A fine day, a good match, and a clear green... make up a golfer's dream of perfect happiness.' The last essential here is always a feature of Prestwick links. The familiar 'Fore' is a word that is almost unknown there. The club has the exclusive rights in an arbitrary way. Needless to say that they are not in the habit of warning pedestrians off the ground, or of refusing the use of the greens to applicants for a day's Golf, still the private character of the links is a guarantee against any outside interference, and the casual pedestrian, aware that he is on the ground by the goodwill of the club, takes care not to interfere with their game.

Prestwick Golf club came early to the front as a promoter of the game. In 1860, it instituted the Open Championship, an institution which has lasted till the present day, and is now likely to be permanent. For eleven years this important event was played over Prestwick alone; but in 1878, as is well known, young Tom Morris by winning the championship belt three times in succession became its possessor; and after being a year in abeyance the meeting was reconstituted under its present conditions, these conditions providing for the event taking place in rotation over Prestwick, St Andrews and Musselburgh.

Prestwick has always taken a leading part in the settlement of important professional matches. The links are as eminently adapted in every way for these contests, and provide as good a test of Golf, as the best links in the kingdom. There is no living golfer of repute among the professionals who has not played in important matches over the ground.

J. M'Bain, *Golf*, (Dean's Champion Handbook), 1897

THE FINEST FOURSOME

The finest foursome of all that I remember was that between Allan [Roberston] and Tom [Morris] against the two Dunns [Willie and James] in the final at North Berwick. It created intense interest in the golfing world of that day, and crowds flocked to North Berwick to see it. I crossed over from Leven (Fife) with my brother James, and remember it well. When I awoke at five o'clock the rain was pouring, and I got up and told my brother so, and that it would be useless to go. However, in a short time afterwards, he came to my bedroom and said 'Man, Tom, I see a wee glint of blue sky! I think we should gang.'

'All right!' I said, 'I'm up.' And in due time we arrived at North Berwick.

On meeting Allan, I said I had come to see him win. He replied that he hoped so; but he had a dejected look about him, and I got the impression that he was doubtful of the result. The match was one of thirty-six holes, which required five or seven rounds (I forget which) of the North Berwick Links at that time, and one hole more.

The match started amidst the greatest enthusiasm. The weather had cleared up, but the wind blew pretty strong from the south-west. Each party had its own tail of supporters, those for the Musselburgh men predominating – for which, of course, the proximity of that place to North Berwick might account. They were led by Gourlay, the ball-maker. I never saw a match where such vehement party spirit was displayed. So great was the keenness and the anxiety to see whose ball had the best lie, that no sooner were the shots played than off the whole crowd ran, helter-skelter; and as one of the other lay best, so demonstrations were made by each party.

Golf on the links at North Berwick, c. 1890, scene of 'the finest foursome'.

Sir David Baird was umpire, and a splendid one he made. He was very tall and so commanded a good view of the field; but it took all his firmness to keep even tolerable order.

The early part of the match went greatly in favour of the Dunns, whose play was magnificent. Their driving, in fact, completely overpowered their opponents. They went sweeping over hazards which the St Andrews men had to play short of. At lunch time the Dunns were four up, and long odds were offered on them.

On resuming the match, the advantage went still further to the credit of the Musselburgh men, and everyone thought that victory was theirs; but one never knows when the tide at golf will turn – and turn it did. Allan warmed up and got more into his game; and then one hole was taken and another and yet another; and I remember Captain Campbell of Schiehallion, with whom I was walking, saying in great glee – 'Gad, sir, if they take another hole they'll win the match!' And, to be sure, another was won, and so on until the match stood all equal and two to play.

How different the attitude of the Dunns' supporters now from their jubilant and vaunting manner at lunch time! Silence reigned, concern was on every brow, the elasticity had completely gone from Gourlay's step, and the profoundest anxiety marked every line of his countenance. The very Dunns themselves were demoralised!

On the other hand, Allan and Tom were serene, and their supporters as lively as they had been depressed before. We felt victory was ours!

When the tee shots were played for the second last hole, off we flew as usual to see whose ball lay best! To our intense dismay Allan's lay very badly, whilst the Dunns' lay further on beautifully. Should the Dunns win this hole they would be DORMY – they might win the match! Our revulsion of feeling was great, and as play proceeded was intensified, for Allan and Tom had played three more with their ball lying in a bunker close to and in front of the putting green!

But, on the other hand, the Dunns' ball was lying close at the back of a curb-stone on a cart track off the green to the right! First of all they wished the stone removed, and called to some one to go for a spade; but Sir David Baird would not sanction its removal, because it was off the course and a fixture. The ball had therefore to be played as it lay. One of the Dunns (I forget which) struck at the ball with his iron but hit the top of the stone. The other did the same; and again the same operation was performed and 'the like' played. All this time the barometer of our expectation had been steadily rising and had now almost reached 'Set Fair!'

The odd had now to be played, and this was done by striking the ball with the back of the iron on to grass beyond the track. Had that been done at first, the hole might have been won and the match also; but both men had by this time lost all judgment and nerve, and played most recklessly. The consequence was the loss of the hole, and Allan and Tom DORMY.

We felt the victory was now secure: and so, in fact, it turned out, and Allan and Tom remained the victors by two holes.

I think it only just to say that, in my opinion, the winning of the above match was due to Tom Morris. Allan was decidedly off his game at the start, and played weakly and badly for a long time – almost justifying the jeers thrown at him, such as 'That wee body in the red jacket canna play gouf', and such like. Tom, on the other hand, played with pluck and determination throughout.

H. Thomas Peter, *Golfing Reminiscences of an Old Hand*, 1890

J. H. TAYLOR v ANDREW KIRKALDY

We played thirty-six holes and Taylor never got a hole in front of me from start to finish, and I never was more than one up. It was neck and neck all the way. The strain was 'gey bad'. There was one hole in the last round where he had a chance. The ground was hard and keen and a little wind was blowing. Both our balls lay on the green, not more than a foot from the hole and perhaps only ten inches. I said 'A half?' to Taylor. 'No, Andrew,' he said. 'You play.' His ball was about an inch in front of mine. I said 'Lift your ball, then.' I played and missed. The ball struck the side of the hole and dribbled a yard past on the keen green. It was like putting on a window.

Taylor must, at that moment, have felt pleased that he decided to play instead of halving the hole. But holes are never lost or won till the ball is out of sight.

It was absurd to think that Taylor would miss a ten-inch putt after I had been daft enough to do it, so I played back to the hole very carelessly, feeling sure that he would get in; in fact I played with one hand on the back of the putter – tempting Providence! Luckily for me I did not miss that careless putt. When Taylor came to play his ten-inch putt we stood as still as tombstones. I cannot tell you what I felt like when he missed and ran two feet past the hole, and then missed again coming back. Of course I was pleased, and I had a right to be, and did not say 'Hard luck!' like a hypocrite...

Watched by the white-bearded 'Old' Tom Morris, Andrew Kirkaldy drives off in a challenge match at St Andrews in 1903. Three other top professionals – Archie Simpson, Ben Sayers and Alex Herd – were involved.

On leaving the sixteenth green we were all even. Both had a satisfactory drive over the Stationmaster's garden going to the seventeenth green – one of the longest holes. Taylor played a fine second shot, his ball resting at the foot of the green. My second was away to the left behind the deep pot bunker. Some of my friends said, 'Pitch it over the bunker, Andrew.' I said, 'I dare not pitch this. If I do I'll put the ball in the road. Taylor has a certain 5 and I must get a 5.'

Mr John Ball, Mr Harold Hilton and Mr John Low and many other leading amateurs of the day were standing by weighing up the position. I noticed a little hollow to the right of the bunker and saw that if I played the shot properly I could cannon against the side and curl in towards the hole. But there was the risk of taking the wrong line and going into the bunker.

'Chance yer luck,' said John Herd, the uncle of Sandy Herd, who was my caddie.

'That's what I like to hear,' said I. 'No bunker-fright for me.' I chanced my luck and it came off. The shot was about twenty yards. I ran it up and the ball came beautifully round the bias of the ground and lay within two inches of the pin. 'Hard luck,' said somebody, thinking how near I was to holing out. But I had nothing to complain of with the ball lying where it did. The very ground seemed to shake with the clapping of the crowd...

We went to the eighteenth tee – the thirty-sixth of the match – and I being dormy crowed over him saying, 'That's the door locked, Taylor; you canna beat me now.' 'True, but I can draw with you, Andrew,' he said. 'It's possible, Taylor,' I replied, 'but I have only to get a half to win and you have to get a win to halve...'

We both had long drives and Taylor's second lay near the green. He played the odd after we measured and almost holed a beautiful mashie pitch – the sort of shot at which he has been the master since that day, twenty-five years ago. The ball looked into the hole. It was the gutta ball, of course, that plays no tricks. My third shot was past the hole about a yard. I was in no hurry or flurry, but just looked and sank the ball, beating the champion by a putt. Taylor shook hands as heartily as if he had won.

Andrew Kirkaldy, *Fifty Years of Golf*, 1921

GOLF PROS

I wonder why all the golf champions that I have known have always been most agreeable men – that is, the professionals. The amateurs, on the other hand, have not always deserved such high praise.

Take James Braid, Sandy Herd, or J. H. Taylor – where will you find better men? I know their companionship does me good, and particularly what I like about them is their keenness – it must be an infernal nuisance for them to play with a bad golfer like myself, yet somehow they give one the impression that they are just as anxious to beat me as if they were playing for the championship.

Once upon a time I went down to Sandwich with the Aga Khan and J. H. Taylor. His Highness was not in form, and was getting depressed. It was summer, and the ground was hard, and as we approached the last green the Aga Khan hit his ball hard on the top and accordingly was stricken with sadness.

Suddenly I heard Taylor's voice saying, 'Really, your Highness, what is the use of my dinning into your ears to pitch the ball up to the hole when these run-up shots come so naturally to you?'

The next day the Aga Khan played very well, and I could not help thinking that Taylor's words of encouragement on the previous day had something to do with it.

Lord Castlerosse, *Valentine's Days*, 1934

'The car park champion' Seve Ballesteros celebrates during the 1979 Open at Lytham St Annes.

SEVE BALLESTEROS

All three of Severiano Ballesteros's victories have been high drama, reflecting the excitement the man creates on a golf course – even if going round in 75. After becoming the youngest Open champion this century, some Americans labelled him 'the car park champion' because his final-round tee shot at Lytham's 16th finished among BBC vehicles. It is true that he hit few fairways and some very wild shots but his powers of recovery were phenomenal and became his trademark.

His victory at St Andrews was different. He hardly dropped a shot to par and this time avoided all the bunkers. With the contest in the balance between the Spaniard and Tom Watson, Ballesteros's finish was decisive. He managed a par at the impossible Road hole and then birdied the last and Latin emotions flowed. Back at Lytham in 1988, he raced into the lead with a 67 in difficult weather but come the final round it was a contest between new leader Nick Price, Ballesteros, Faldo and Lyle. The last two eventually faded and Ballesteros seized the title with a course record of 65.

By winning the 1980 Masters, Ballesteros heralded a new era that has seen a steady shift of power from America to Europe. He added another Masters title in 1983 and can number 63 wins worldwide, many of them on the hugely successful European Tour. Whether smiling or scowling, he remains – like Arnold Palmer with whom he is so often compared – the star attraction.

Michael Hobbs, *British Open Champions*, 1991

NICK FALDO

With four major championships to his credit, Faldo can well claim to be the greatest British player since the far-off days of the Great Triumvirate. Those who would point to the name of Cotton should note that he seldom cared to compete in the United States and his achievements there were negligible.

There are strong contrasts in the ways that Faldo has won his majors. At Muirfield in 1987 he ground out a round with every hole in par and was 'given' that Open when Paul Azinger collapsed on the last two holes. His consecutive victories in the Masters also had an element of chance. In 1989, during the sudden-death play-off, Scott Hoch missed a tiny putt for victory and the following year Ray Floyd pulled an iron shot into water at the same stage. Faldo's finest hour to date is undoubtedly his Open victory at St Andrews. After a brilliant start of 67, 65 he was tied for the lead with Greg Norman and then destroyed him with a 67 to the Australian's 76. On the final day Faldo was faced with the prospect of ludicrous failure if he had thrown away his five-stroke lead but his play was unwavering.

Much has been made of Faldo's swing changes and it was certainly courageous

Nick Faldo nearing the end of his final round in the 1987 Open at Muirfield. He 'ground out' his victory over Paul Azinger with 18 straight pars to win his first Major title.

to risk losing his game altogether. We shall never know if he would have won those majors with his old swing. However, his short-game skills have been equally valuable in taking him to the very top.

Michael Hobbs, *British Open Champions*, 1991

A STORMY MEETING

A fierce nor'-wester with driving rain and wrack usually applies an effective closure on the links. What old St Andrews golfer but can recall the dispiriting spectacle of the long-ago coterie of caddies – Watties, Willies, and Tams – slouching at the gable end of the Golf Hotel, and taking an occasional look 'out into the west', in the hope of a rift in the murk that would prognosticate a round in the afternoon?

'Most disthrashful' was the common opinion on the morning of the 28th when 'Old Tom' placed the ball and Mr W. J. Mure struck it off to officially open the Autumn Meeting of 1898. The players who came early in the draw were, of course, out to witness the formal function, and with them a handful of lady devotees, sombrely arrayed – a brave little gallery of the fair, which faded away like a vision the instant the gun-fire intimated that play had commenced. A thin, dark line of the smaller caddies hung very patiently in the vicinity of the road, waiting to pounce on the captain's first ball, and obtain the customary honorarium; one or two of the deep-thinking sort giving a liberal margin for a pull or a slice. The coveted trophy fell into the hands of a namesake of the new 'Horace', but he had to measure his length in the muddy roadway before securing it.

The gay bunting on the staff fronting the Union Parlour blustered about wildly and wetly, the Royal Standard at the mast-head, and the club's colours at the yard-arm, a red-and-blue cross quartering the final and making place for the Union Jack, the Crown, the transverse clubs, and the St Andrew's Cross – the whole frayed and faded from the effects of previous similar celebrations.

Beyond the heavy curtain of clouds, as the afternoon revealed the peaks of the Grampians, from 'the steep, frowning glories of dark Lochnagar' to the ptarmigan range of the Glas-meol, where the speckled birds were hiding among the grey-lichened stones, were sprinkled with snow, the first sign of the year's advancing age. Seaward, the only vessel visible in the offing was a gallant steam-yacht lying by, while the noble owner, with a handicap of ten strokes, made good his claim to first place in the club's sweepstake.

'Old Tom', the presiding genius of the game, hale and hearty, none ever more so, sent off the gross of players, with a pleasant word to friends old and new – marvellously cheerful, with his macintosh well up over his ears. He scouted the suggestion that a pocket-pistol was the proper weapon to start off the day's aspirants on their stormy career. He had often seen wilder weather, but there would be nothing under eighty on this occasion. Jimmy Morris, who seldom sets foot on the links, and yet keeps a watchful eye on them, allowed one stroke more, but the issue showed the wisdom of the elder's opinion. The veteran greenkeeper could tell of the year when, driving in from the fourth hole, Major Bethune's ball was blown back by a fierce nor'-easter behind the teeing-ground – a very retrogressive mode of procedure, that must have called out the utmost powers of the skilled military strategist. Tom could tell besides of that other year when, in the midst of a gale, Admiral Maitland Dougal of Scotscraig, went out in the lifeboat to the rescue of a shipwrecked crew, and at the close of the same afternoon handed in the winning card.

We used to hear the 'Rook' tell of 'Goufin' Charley's' hardihood one medal day on the North Inch: how, when none others would risk the effects of a steady downpour, he pulled off his coat, buckled up his sleeves, and made good his title to the club's blue ribbon, driving home to Buttergask at least with a dry coat on his back, and, what was of chiefest importance, the medal in the pocket.

But, distracting as was the weather on the 28th, the cards were by no means unworthy of an Autumn Meeting. On the contrary, the adverse conditions only served to mark the lower scores as specially brilliant, and M. De Zoete's name was added to the 'Royal and Ancient' list of winners under circumstances that proved his form to be exceptionally fine. He had but a handful of followers, while some of the old favourites were more highly favoured; but, according to their degree, his partisans gave him a well-merited ovation when he holed out on the last green.

'Who is he?' we asked some bystanders, when an authority of repute gave us the negative information, 'No one knows anything about him'; but before the day was out everyone in St Andrews knew at least something about him.

The redoubtable Mr F. G. Tait and the perennial Mr Balfour-Melville were but two strokes behind, and took another day to settle their title. These all played when the gale was still high, and the velocity of the wind will be best understood when it is stated that one of the scratch players, playing from the tee to the last hole, and, no doubt, fearing to be trapped in the ruts, elected to drive with his cleek, and reached within a yard or two of the road.

The same player, Mr Fergusson, *held* a very useful putt at the 'Corner o' the Dyke', playing in the foursome of the afternoon. Messrs Tait and Burn had the better of the game until then, and with three to play, stood two up, their ball on the green, and their opponents' bunkered at the edge of it, and the latter pair called to give the odd. Mr Laidlay made very sure of being out, though compelled to play at right angles to the hole; whereupon his partner, in playing two more, did full amends for his faulty approach, by running down a twenty-yards putt, so serving to keep the match open. Coming at the time it did, it saved a hopeless-looking contest, and must have compensated largely for the disappointment of the forenoon. Mr Tait failed to do the needful with a short putt at the road, and, as his partner repaid him by a slight error of judgment at the close, they had to content themselves with the half of a match that looked like a certainty four holes from home – another illustration of the glorious uncertainties of golf.

During the day the large oil-painting, by Dickensen, of the more notable present members of the club was on view in the writing-room, and came in for a considerable amount of favourable criticism from both members and friends. The grouping and toning are exceedingly good, and many of the portraits are first-rate, both in likeness and pose. Some of the figures have been familiar forms on the links for well-nigh half-a-century, and among the old generation of players one can readily pick out such veterans as Mr Gilbert Mitchell-Innes, Dr Argyle Robertson, Major Bethune, besides the non-player and club's chaplain, the Very Reverend Dr Boyd, who occupies a modest position in the rear of the group.

We miss, of course, one once familiar figure, long associated with the old race of players, and connected with the finest traditions of the game, an ornament of the links both in face and form, the late Lieut.-Col. Boothby. The players who have reached the middle distance of life have representatives equally recognisable in such portraits as those of Lord Kingsburgh, Mr Arthur Balfour, and Dr Lang; while in the foreground there is a capital group of present-day leaders of the field, whose praise is in the mouth of all golfers.

In all, there are nearly two hundred figures on the canvas, and what strikes one as marking a change in the haberdashery of the game, is the scarcity of scarlet, a mere tithe affecting the colours of the club, and, for the rest, each one has been a law unto himself.

At half-past four the little piece of ordnance announced that the competitive part of the programme had been completed, and soon after, as if in honour of the occasion, the westering sun shone out, and the evening sky began to glow with wonderful combinations of deep scarlet and blue. The leaden clouds rolled away, giving place to an illumination of especial brilliancy, and the weather-wise, always at hand with the pat proverbial saw or couplet, repeated the lines of the dramatist...

'The sun hath made a golden set,
And, by the bright track of his fiery car,
Gives promise of a better day to-morrow.'

And so it was; for we awoke next morning to another fresh and bright September day – a further instalment of our Indian summer – and the waves, instead of rolling up against the blast, with the spray driven from their crests like clouds of snowdrift, ran rippling brightly over the tawny sand. The brown fishing-boats sailed peacefully back and forward in the bay, for Boreas had retired to some icy cavern among his native fields of snow, seeming to feel like the brawny blacksmith of baritone notoriety, that

'Something attempted, something done,
Had earned a *day's* repose.'

The Golfer's Magazine, November 1898

A STAGE FOR LEADING LADIES

I must call a halt somewhere, but there is one more match that must be mentioned, a match not between men but between ladies, the final of the Ladies' Championship at Troon in 1925 between Miss Joyce Wethered and Miss Cecil Leitch. It contained every possible dramatic element except the international one. It was perhaps as well that this was absent. As it was the crowd was so great and so much excited that the player had scarcely finished her stroke when she was swallowed up in a hot seething mass of humanity.

From the very beginning of the Championship this match had been anticipated. Miss Leitch had been for a long time the undisputed queen of golf, but then an even greater than her had arisen in Miss Wethered. She in her turn had reigned since their meeting at Prince's in 1922. Now that Miss Wethered was in one half of the draw and Miss Leitch in the other there was a chance of another final between them. Both parties have the power of inspiring almost fanatical enthusiasm among their supporters, and excitement was at boiling point. Yet on the eve of the final it was difficult to imagine that the match would really be a match at all. Miss Wethered's progress had been a series of executions carried out with merciful swiftness. Round after round she had clung to an average of fours on this long and testing course. Miss Glenna Collett, the American champion and a very fine player,

Joyce Wethered and Glenna Collett prior to the final of the 1929 British Ladies Championship at St Andrews. Watched by over 5,000 people, Wethered came out of retirement to beat her American rival with a hole to spare.

had held her for a while, but in the end had been overwhelmed like the others by that remorseless accuracy. Miss Leitch, on the other hand, had not been herself at all. She had never touched her proper form, she had only got through by her great powers of fighting and because some of her opponents had been so terrified at the chance of beating her that they could not take what the gods gave them; she had appeared ill at ease and anxious, always brave but never confident.

And then on the morrow all was changed and a new Miss Leitch appeared, calm and serene, having reached the place that she had set out to reach, 'Her cares dropped from her like the needles shaken from out the gusty pine.'

She was ready to do battle for her life, and she did it so magnificently that, though in the end she lost the match, it was she rather than her conqueror that was the heroine of the day. Everybody knew that she would rise to the occasion and make a great effort, but hardly anyone, I think, expected quite such a great one.

From the very beginning of that match Miss Leitch played like her best self, confidently and boldly. As for Miss Wethered, though she did not wilt under the fierce attack, something of the divine fire had temporarily departed, and so at the end of ten holes we were faced with the almost incredible situation that Miss Wethered was three down. Then, however, she made her great push. She played grandly and finally holed a long putt on the home green to be home in 35 and square the match. Miss Leitch had never weakened for a single moment: she had played as well as ever and had given no openings. To lose three holes to such golf was almost inevitable and probably any other lady golfer would have lost several more.

They were at it hammer and tongs again after luncheon, with the same fine golf. Any notion of Miss Wethered's going right away had long since been dispelled. Going to the ninth hole she was one down and there came one of the crises of the match. Miss Wethered had a putt for the hole, but she was stymied. To go for the shot and knock her enemy's ball in would be to be two down and that would be a very serious situation indeed. To go for it and bring it off would not only mean the gain of a valuable hole but would almost inevitably have a moral effect. She took the brave risk, lofted the shot perfectly, won the hole and squared the match.

The moral effect was palpable enough. For the next six holes Miss Wethered dominated the play. She was two up with three to go; if she could put a fairly long iron shot on to the sixteenth green she would in all human probability win the match by 3 and 2. This was the type of shot that she had been playing better perhaps then all the rest. Every one had so intense a belief in her that even at this most critical moment hardly a soul doubted that she would put the ball bang in the middle of the green. For once, however, she was not straight, but hooked the ball into the rough mounds on the left of the green. The hole was halved and Miss Leitch was still alive.

Again the moral effect was obvious. Miss Wethered for once played two weak holes in succession, played them as if she was shaken and tired. Miss Leitch metaphorically leaped on her like a tigress and, aided at the last hole by a little of that fortune that aids the brave, most gloriously squared the match. And that ought to be the end of the story. A half was the right ending; the greatest thirty-seventh hole in the world must have seemed a pity. However, they had to go on, someone had to win, and the someone was Miss Wethered, who laid a very long putt stone dead at the thirty-seventh. It was a fine effort and deserved victory, but every one who saw that match will always wish that there could for that year have been two queens on twin thrones of exactly equal splendour.

Bernard Darwin, *Green Memories*, 1928

PILGRIMAGE TO ST ANDREWS

It has frequently been observed that St Andrews is to the golfer what Mecca is to the Mohammedan. The comparison is apt in many respects. The Mohammedan turns his face towards Mecca when he prays, and gives utterance to words

The Grand Old Man of Golf, Tom Morris Snr, at his beloved St Andrews c. 1895.

expressive of his belief in the Prophet. The golfer turns his thoughts towards St Andrews. Each of their kind holds his duty to be sacred in the eyes of true disciples. Both places too are reached by a certain pilgrimage, and, when the desired haven is attained, the happy pilgrim forgets all but the supreme delight of the moment.

St Andrews having been reached, and the gauntlet of the younger fry of the caddie tribe having been run, the first thing to do was, of course, to visit the shrine of that deity of the place, Tom Morris, who received his visitors with the genial cordiality which has made him more than esteemed by all who have come into contact with him.

J.A., *Golf,* 1892

THE TRIUMVIRATE

There is a natural law in games by which, periodically, a genius arises and sets the standard of achievement perceptibly higher than ever before. He forces the pace; the rest have to follow as best they can, and end by squeezing out of themselves just a yard or two more than they would have believed possible.

During the last year or two we have seen this law at work in billiards. Lindrum has set up a new standard in scoring power and our players, in trying to live up to him, have excelled their old selves. The same thing has happened from time to time in golf, and those whom we call The Triumvirate undoubtedly played their part in the 'speeding up' of the game.

Taylor, though by a few months the youngest of the three, was the first to take the stage, and it has always been asserted that he first made people realise what was possible in combined boldness and accuracy in playing the shots up to the pin. Anything in the nature of safety play in approaching became futile when there was a man who could play brassie shots to the flag in the manner of mashie shots. Mr Hilton has suggested that this raising of the standard really began earlier and was due to another great Englishman, Mr John Ball. It may well be so, for it is hard to imagine anything bolder or straighter than that great golfer's shots to the green, but Taylor, being the younger man and coming later, burst on a much larger golfing world than had Mr Ball. Moreover, he was a professional who played here, there and everywhere, and so was seen by a large number of golfers, whereas the great amateur, except at championship times, lay comparatively hidden at Hoylake. Time was just ripe when Taylor appeared: golf was 'booming' and the hour and the man synchronised. Though in the end he failed in his first championship at Prestwick, he had done enough to show that he was going to lead golfers a dance to such a measure as they had not yet attempted. In the next year he won, and for two years after that the world struggled to keep up with him as best it could.

Then there arose somebody who could even improve on Taylor. This was Harry Vardon, who tied with him in the third year of his reign (1896) and beat him on playing off. There was an interval of one more year before the really epoch-making character of Vardon was appreciated. Then he won his second championship in 1898 and was neither to hold nor to bind. He devastated the country in a series of triumphal progresses and, in the case of Lindrum, there was no doubt that a greater than all before him had come. To the perfect accuracy of Taylor he added a perceptible something more of power and put the standard higher by at least one peg.

And, it may be asked, did Braid have no effect? I hardly think he did in the same degree though he was such a tremendous player. He took longer to mature than did his two contemporaries. Of all men he seemed intended by nature to batter the unresponsive gutty to victory, and he won one championship with a gutty, but his greatest year, his real period of domination, came with the rubber core. He cannot be said to have brought in a new epoch except to this extent perhaps, that he taught people to realise that putting could be learned by hard toil. He disproved the aphorism that putting is an inspiration for, after having been not far short of an execrable putter, he made himself, during his conquering period, into as effective a putter as there was in the country. By doing so he brought new hope to many who had thought that a putter must be born not made and had given it up as a bad job.

Presumably everybody thinks that his own youth was spent in the golden age, and that the figures of that period were more romantic than those of any other. At any rate I can claim romance and to spare for my early years of grown-up golf, for I went up to Cambridge in 1894 and that was the year of Taylor's first win at Sandwich. Moreover, The Triumvirate were then, I am sure, far more towering figures in the public eye than are their successors of today. It was their good fortune to have no rivals from beyond the sea. They were indisputably the greatest in the world. Then, too, they had so few ups and downs. Today a professional is in the limelight one year and in almost the dreariest of shade the next, but these three, by virtue of an extraordinary consistency always clustered round the top. Finally their zenith was the zenith of the exhibition match. They were constantly playing against one another and no matter on what mud-heap they met, the world really cared which of them won.

It is partly no doubt because I was in the most hero-worshipping stage of youth (I have never wholly emerged from it) but it is also largely due to the personalities of those great players that I can remember quite clearly the first occasion on which I saw each of them. It is a compliment my memory can pay to very few others. Taylor I first saw at Worlington (better, perhaps, known as Mildenhall) when he came almost in the first flush of his champion's honours, to play Jack White, who was then the professional there. I can see one or two shots that he played that day just as clearly as any that I have watched in the thirty-seven years since. I had seen several good Scottish professionals play before that, including my earliest hero, Willie Fernie, most graceful and dashing of golfers. I thought I knew just what a professional style was like, but here was something quite new to me. Here was a man who seemed to play his driver after the manner of a mashie. There was no tremendous swing, no glorious follow-through. Jack White, with his club, in those days, sunk well home into the palm of his right hand, was the traditional free Scottish slasher. He was driving the ball as I imagined driving. Taylor was altogether different and his style reminded me of a phrase in the Badminton book, which I knew by heart, about Jamie Anderson and his 'careless little switch'. One has grown used to J. H. long since, but the first view of him was intensely striking, and I am inclined to think that in his younger days he stood with his right foot more forward than he does now, so that the impression of his playing iron shots with his driver was the more marked. He was not appallingly long, but he was appallingly straight, and he won a very fine match at the thirty-fifth hole.

The Great Triumvirate at Aberlady, near Muirfield, in 1906 just before the Open. Harry Vardon (standing, right), J.H. Taylor (seated, back right) and James Braid (seated, front right). Braid, who won that year's Open, suffered from severe motion sickness so never himself owned a car.

Incidentally, the memory of that game makes me realise how much the rubber cored-ball has changed golf. The first hole at Worlington was much what it is today, except that the green was the old one on the right. Now the aspiring Cambridge undergraduate calls it a two-shot hole and is disappointed with a five there. On that day, to be sure it was against a breeze – Taylor and Jack White took three wooden club shots apiece to reach the outskirts of the green, and Taylor with a run up and a putt won it in five against six.

My first sight of Vardon came next. It was on his own course at Ganton, whither I went for the day from Whitby, and he had just won his first championship. He was always playing an ordinary game and I only saw one or two shots, including his drive to the first hole. Two memories vividly remain. One was that he was wearing trousers and that from that day to this I have never seen him play except in knickerbockers, an attire which he first made fashionable amongst his brother professionals. The other is that his style seemed, as had Taylor's on a first view, entirely unique. The club appeared contrary to all orthodox teaching, to be lifted up so very straight. Even now, when I have seen him play hundreds and hundreds of shots, I cannot quite get it out of my head that he did in those early days take up the club a little more abruptly than he did later. The ball flew away very high, with an astonishing ease, and he made the game look more magical and unattainable than anyone I had ever seen. For that matter, I think he does so still.

'By their modesty and dignity and self-respect, they helped make the professional golfer a very different person' – Harry Vardon and James Braid, Coventry, 1912.

In view of later events it is curious to recall that a good local amateur, Mr Broadwood, who was playing with him, talked then of his putting as the most heart-breaking part of his game, and said that he holed everything. I only saw one putt and that he missed.

It must have been a year later that there came the first vision of the third member of The Triumvirate, who had hardly then attained that position. This was at Penarth, where there was a Welsh championship meeting, and Taylor and Herd were to play an exhibition match. Taylor could not come; at the last moment Braid was sent for to take his place and arrived late the night before. I remember that he did in his youthful energy what I feel sure he has not done for a long time now; he went out early after breakfast to have a look at the course and play some practice shots. His enemy, by the way, had come a whole day early and played a couple of rounds. I have almost entirely forgotten the Penarth course, and the shots I played on it myself; the one thing I can vaguely remember is the look of the first hole and of Braid hitting those shots towards it. Here was something much more in the manner that one had been brought up to believe orthodox, but with an added power; save for Mr Edward Blackwell, with whom I had once had the honour of playing, I had never seen anyone hit so malignantly hard at the ball before. Mr Hutchinson's phrase about his 'divine fury' seemed perfectly apposite. One imagined that there was a greater chance of some error on an heroic scale than in the case of Taylor and Vardon, and so indeed there was, but I remember no noble hooks that day, nothing but a short putt or two missed when he had a winning lead so that Herd crept a little nearer to him.

From the time when I was at Cambridge till I sold my wig in 1908, my golfing education was neglected for, if I may so term it, my legal one. I played all the golf I could, which was a good deal, but watched hardly any. Therefore I never – sad to say – saw Vardon in his most dominating era, not the great foursome match over four different courses in which he and Taylor crushed Braid and Herd, chiefly through one terrific landslide of holes at Troon. However, in the end I managed to see each of the three win two championships, Braid at Prestwick and St Andrews in 1908 and 1910, Taylor at Deal and Hoylake, 1909 and 1913, Vardon at Sandwich and Prestwick, 1911 and 1914. I suppose the most exciting was in 1914 when Vardon and Taylor, leading the field, were drawn together on the last day, and the whole of the West of Scotland was apparently moved with a desire to watch them. Braid, too, played his part on that occasion, for had he not designed the bunker almost in the middle of the fairway at the fourth hole? And was it not fear of that bunker that drove Taylor too much to the right into the other one by the Pow Burn, so that he took a seven? No wonder J. H. said that the man who made that bunker should be buried in it with a niblick through his heart. Yes, that was a tremendous occasion, and Braid's golf in 1908 – 291 with an eight in it at the Cardinal – was incredibly brilliant; and Vardon's driving when he beat Massy in playing off the tie at Sandwich was, I think, the most beautiful display of wooden club hitting I ever saw; but for sheer thrilling quality give me Taylor at Hoylake in 1913. There was no great excitement since, after qualifying by the skin of his teeth, he won by strokes and strokes; but I have seen nothing else in golf which so stirred me and made me want to cry. The wind and the rain were terrific, but not so terrific as Taylor, with his cap pulled down, buffeting his way through them. There are always one or two strokes which stick faster in the memory than any others, and I noticed the other day that my friend Mr Macfarlane recalled just the one that I should choose. It was the second shot played with a cleek to the Briars hole in the very teeth of the storm. I can still see Taylor standing on rock-like feet, glued flat on the turf, watching that ball as it whizzes over the two cross bunkers straight for the green. There never was such a cleek shot; there never will be such another as long as the world stands.

It is surely a curious fact that, though these three players dominated golf for so long, and the golfer is essentially an imitative animal, no one of them has been the founder of a school. They made people play better by having to live up to their standard, but they did not make people play like them. Here are three strongly marked and characteristic styles to choose from, and yet where are their imitators? Vardon had one, to be sure, in Mr A. C. Lincoln, an excellent player who belonged to Totteridge; he had at any rate many of the Vardonian mannerisms and a strong superficial likeness. There is George Duncan, too, with a natural talent for mimicry; he remodelled the swing he had learned in Scotland after he first saw the master. Imagine Duncan slowed down and there is much of Vardon. Beyond those two, I can think of no one in the least like him. It is much the same with Taylor. His two sons, J. H., Jr. and Leslie, have something of the tricks of the backswing, but nobody has got the flat-footed hit and the little grunt that goes with it. Braid, with that strange combination of a portentous gravity and a sudden, furious lash seems the most impossible model of all. I know no one who has even copied his waggle, with that little menacing shake of the clubhead in the middle of it. Each of the three was so unlike the other two that the world hesitated which model to take and ended by taking none. American players look as if they had all been cast in one admirable mould. Ours look as if they came out of innumerable different ones, and as if in nearly every mould there had been some flaw. It was part of the fascination of The Triumvirate that each was extraordinarily individual, but now it seems almost a pity for British golf. If only just one of them could have been easier to imitate! In other respects, of course, they did all three of them leave a model which could be imitated. By all the good golfing qualities of courage and sticking power and chivalry, by their modesty and dignity and self-respect, they helped to make the professional golfer a very different person from what he was when they first came on the scene. Their influence as human beings has been as remarkable as their achievements as golfers.

Bernard Darwin, *Out of the Rough*, 1932

WOOSNAM WINS THE US MASTERS

Up ahead Jose-Maria Olazabal was in trouble. He had gone from the fairway bunker on the 72nd hole of Augusta National to the bunker by the green.

Back on the tee, Ian Woosnam was in torment. He knew that the Spaniard's erratic progress meant that a par would probably give him his first major championship, the US Masters. The problem was how to get it.

He asked his caddie Phil Mobley how far it was to the fairway bunkers. The question came out as a croak. Throat and tongue dried by the tension, Mobley told him the distance.

Then Woosnam had his moment of inspiration. 'How far is it,' he asked, 'to *carry* those bunkers?' Mobley, good caddie that he is, quickly worked it out. 'It's 268 yards,' he said, 'to get over the lot.'

In those moments Woosnam and Mobley had initiated a new strategy for playing the 18th at Augusta. There was nothing subtle about it; just blast the ball as hard as possible left, going left.

'I know,' says Woosnam, 'that when I hit it as hard as I can the ball will either go straight or draw. It's natural to my swing. So when I saw Ollie [playing up ahead] in the bunker and then my playing partner Tom Watson went into the trees on the right, I decided to go as far left as I could. There's nothing over there except the members' practice area [which is in bounds but was crammed with spectators] and the only possible problem would be if a spectator walked off with my ball.'

Woosnam, one of the game's longest hitters, launched himself – and hit it perfectly. As it rocketed off the tee the American television commentators immediately went into their 'Uh, oh' routine, thinking it was headed for the sand. They were astonished when it cleared everything, and so were the marshalls, who had not anticipated this new tactic.

The ball hurtled into a crowd of, literally, thousands, coming to rest on trampled grass. Woosnam had negotiated the first, and the worst, of the obstacles of the 18th hole.

Looking back at that act, after a year to think about it, Olazabal is almost in awe of Woosnam's tee-shot. 'I had never even thought of that route. I could not do that. Once you are there, of course, it is perfect, but...'

It is difficult even now to persuade the Spaniard to talk about that last hole. So much happened to him that he feels was unfair. 'I hit a good solid tee-shot to the left centre of the fairway; it never moved in the air but when it landed it kicked left into the bunker. Then it was a seven-iron distance, but I was up against the face and had to take an eighth; I hit it good, it pitched over the bunker by the green, and then it spins back into the sand. It was a rough bunker-shot but I hit it to 12 feet, before it came back and back, 40 feet away...'

Three good, solid shots, three poor results. He took a bogey five and knew as he walked from the green that his first chance of a major championship had almost certainly been taken from him.

Back down the fairway Woosnam was surrounded by bewildered spectators and frantic marshalls. In order for the Welshman to play his second they would have to clear away several thousand people and, as Woosnam says, 'they had no idea what

Ian Woosnam holing his final putt to win the 1991 US Masters.

they were doing. I had to join in, shout at people, which was the last thing I wanted in that situation.'

Even after five minutes of jostling he had only succeeded in clearing enough space to swing a club, with a narrow sightline through the crowds. 'I couldn't see the green; I couldn't even see the stands. I had to aim at a particular tree on the treeline 100 yards past the green.'

But all he had in his hands was an eight-iron; the lie was reasonable and he told himself to remember only the hours of practice. 'I knew I could do it with my eyes shut, which was just as well since it was a blind shot anyway.'

The shot was almost perfect. With another yard in length it would have been, but it finished just off the putting surface, leaving him with what in any other circumstances would have been a simple chip. He got it six feet past the hole and then, with that huge right uppercut, urged his ball into the hole.

Olazabal had watched the proceedings from the scorers' tent at the back of the green. When Woosnam's putt went in he was devastated. 'For me it was the first time I had felt I could win a major. One par at the last and I would be in the play-off, and I would not be afraid of anyone in a play-off.'

How upset was he? 'I cannot answer that. There are no words. But for months after that I was trying to make up to myself the disappointment. I was trying to hit perfect shots all the time, to try to win, to fill that hole.

'It was worse that it had happened at Augusta, the No. 1 course for me in the world. The skill that every player has can be seen at Augusta; it demands all the shots; nothing is taken away from you. If you have skill and imagination you can show it at Augusta.'

David Davies, *Guardian*, April 1992

KINGS AND QUEENS OF SCOTLAND

There are in Great Britain to-day one thousand, seven hundred and thirty-five golf courses. More are in process of construction, of which some are on the point of completion.

Very many of these are really famous. Some for their great age and traditions – they have been playing continuously on the Royal Dornoch Links, for example, since 1609; some because of their difficulties and fearsome hazards – the rushes at Westward Ho!, 'the Himalayas' at Prestwick, the seventeenth on the Old Course at St Andrews – and because many a Championship has been won and lost there; and some because of the beauties that nature has bestowed upon them.

All the famous courses have marked characteristics peculiarly their own. Many of the little known are as delightful to play over as the illustrious ones. But, in my humble judgment, no keen golfer's education is quite complete – if it ever is! – until he has played upon the King's Course and the Queen's Course at Gleneagles in Perthshire, Scotland.

This somewhat superlative statement is not made without good reason. We in the United States pay a great deal of attention and respect to the opinions of Scottish Professionals; partly because most of us have at some time or another learned the rudiments of the game at their patient hands, and also because they appreciate good golf when they see it. Therefore, one of the reasons why every

'One of the finest courses in the world', King's at Gleneagles.

golfer visiting Scotland should visit Gleneagles is because many Scotch Professionals whom I have spoken to about it have given it as their considered opinion that the King's Course represents one of the finest courses in the world.

It must be a very material, unimaginative player not to find his or her attention wandering here and there from the matter of the score in hand to the landscape and all that it offers. A dozen larks rise throatily and sombre blue-grey mountains tower above you. Trout rise with a 'plop' in streams to your left. Purple and canary heather stretches away and away to your right. Beneath you is the billiard green grass. Beyond is the forget-me-not blue sky, with a white powder puff or cloud drifting vaguely across. And before you are fresh holes of a fascinating nature to conquer. Behind you are regal holes that, alas, have conquered you.

Never at any time during the unforgettable round are you harried by the propinquity of your fellow creatures. So planned is the place that each hole seems a thing apart. Men and women appear upon the sky line here and there, but never to your discomfiture; you scarcely notice them.

You may play a good round or a bad; bad if you are temperamental and 'subject to scenery'; good if you can steel your eyes and your hand to the business of the moment, which is to do justice to these grand golfing holes, and to the card that allows you 80 of a score. You wander back to the little grey stone club house, or to the hotel itself, to the well earned lunch, thinking over some of the gems and how you handled them. Holes, for instance, like 'The Whaup's Nest', one hundred and sixty five yards only, and how you insisted on the Jigger, disbelieving the caddies who proffered the driver because of the head wind, and how woefully short you were! And 'The Wee Bogle', another little fellow, the littlest, one hundred and twenty five yards only; a perfect mashie shot which must be pitched well up. You were short, and the voracious bunker swallowed it. But heavens! What a superb hole.

Then the quiet afternoon on the Queen's. Shorter, but with all the feminine subtleties. Elated by a goodish morning card you set out to vanquish her the more easily. Beware of her guile. For she has devilments of nerve-shattering nature. The 'Witches' Bowster', for example, where you can – and did – slice into the loch. The 'Lover's Gait', where she offered you a 4 and you squandered a scuffling 6 upon her. The 'Needle E'e'... The 'Heather Bell'; they were all as pleasing as their names imply. What a day; what golf; what an evening and a night to come!

Yes, because the sun is now upon its golden journey down towards the sage green and ebony-black of the great hills. Pompous enough they seemed by day; very regal and dignified and sad have they now become. *The Nunc Dimittis* of the day is at hand. Fling wide your bedroom window and gaze upon its pageantry, the like of which you have never seen.

No matter what manner of man or woman you are, you will, and must, be impressed beyond mere speech. The whole barbaric splendour of Scotland appears to be spread before you. Fifty miles of her fair country is presented to your gaze. Mysterious mountain, wandering moorland, gingling burn. And brooding over all that peace of evening, everything is very still. The world seems to have stopped. Colour merges into colour. Here great stains of olive-green gorse; there orange and purple splashes of heather; an infinity of greys, umbers and duns, with the black knife-edge of the mountains cutting into the rose-pink and silver of the skies.

And then there is the faint tinkle of a plate from some remote nether region, recalling you to the mundane matter of food, preceded by the delicious ritual of the 'after exercise' bath and the settling into the cool dress shirt. The cocktail in the American Bar, an interesting place where one is prone to linger. Dinner: a dance or two; complete contentment.

It is supposed, and in most cases very readily – but I cannot help thinking, and indeed I have heard widely travelled Americans say – that there is little further one can go on the road to '100% efficiency' than the appointments and administration of this gargantuan railway Golf hotel resort. It is certainly an example to all Europe. Sumptuous is a fitting term for its appearance, and its achievement. There's a prevailing note of cheerfulness, and a quiet undercurrent of perfect service.

Further, you will get something else as well; something peculiarly your own, which cannot be imitated or surpassed. You will get, in the pearly, early morning, at the height of blazing mid-day, at sunset, and under the benediction of pale moons that wonderful and ever changing picture of Scottish scenery at its best; than which there is surely nothing more impressive?

'Traveller', *The American Golfer*, 1928

THE HOME OF GOLF

In a book about Golf no apology is required for introducing some remarks upon St Andrews. Golf without St Andrews would be almost as intolerable as St Andrews without Golf. For here are the head-quarters of the 'royal, ancient, irritating sport'. Here Tom Morris holds his court, his courtier, the clubmen and the caddies; his throne, the evergreen links; and his sceptre, a venerable putter. Here the children make their entrance into the world, not with silver spoons in their mouths, but with diminutive golf-clubs in their hands. Here the Champion is as much a hero as the greatest general who ever returned in triumph from the wars. Here, in short, is an asylum for golfing maniacs and the happy hunting-ground of the duffer, who, armed with a rusty cleek, sallies forth to mutilate the harmless turf.

Here, there, and everywhere Golf is spreading: almost every day we hear of Tom Morris opening a new green and declaring it (with a faithless regularity) to be 'the finest green in the country' – though he will occasionally modify the statement to this extent, that it is 'second only to St Andrews'.

There are links which are sporting, and links which are long: links which have good putting greens, and links which have none at all: links which have no hazards,

'In St Andrews are the hopes of the golfer fixed.' The legendary 17th and 18th holes on the Old Course.

and links which are all hazard: but place any of them beside St Andrews, and – oh, the difference! In short, St Andrews is the home and nursery of Golf.

In St Andrews are the hopes of the golfer fixed. The very air seems to be impregnated with the spirit of the game. At the tee with the brave old towers behind, the rolling waters of the Bay to the right, and in front the mounds, and hillocks, and levels of the links, one feels that he has reached the end of his pilgrimage to the Shrine of Golf. A new glamour is thrown about the game: the Golfer's 'spirit leaps within him to be gone before him then': he may foozle on the green under the critical eye of a by-standing professional, but 'his heart's his own, his will is free'. And standing at the end hole with his round half accomplished, he can survey the towers of the ruined Cathedral and the ragged masonry of the Castle, and the grey old city itself with the feeling of one who has found life worth living and Golf a game for men.

Robert Barclay, *A Batch of Golfing Papers*, 1892

SPOONS, NIBLICKS AND STYMIES

What chess is to draughts, what billiards is to bagatelle, what cricket is to trap-and-ball, so is golf to hockey. It is a game of skill, judgment, and science. It takes the player to breezy moors and healthful commons; it exhilarates without fatiguing him.

I well remember that inspiriting day when I accompanied those two old friends, members of the renowned and ancient club of St Andrews, to witness their sport and to receive a few practical lessons on the art of avoiding hazards and getting out of a bunker. I well remember the smile of the attendant caddie as I swung the play-club as if I was going to send the ball the famed ten score yards, and only succeeded in 'topping' it after all. It requires practice and patience to acquire the 'far and sure' stroke which is the motto of the best golf players.

Come, then, to the sandy links, as they are called. Their fellows in England are the undulating downs and grassy commons, a plain of fine green turf, diversified by knolls, furze-bushes, tufts of grass, hollows, and, may be, cart-ruts or pools of water. These form in golfer's parlance hazards, which are to be avoided if possible. The caddie is but the Scotch term for club-bearer, and he carries the somewhat miscellaneous appliances which the game demands.

Before, however, the game can be understood, some idea must be formed of the implements with which the game is played.

The Ball is made of gutta-percha, about two inches in diameter, and painted white, so as to be easily seen. Formerly it was made of leather, stuffed hard with feathers. The price is about a shilling.

The Clubs are, however, the most important portion of the golfer's outfit. They are as various as the days in the week, and no good player would begin without a set of at least half a dozen. A fastidious player on an unknown ground would at least have half as many more, and would display with pride his (1) *play-club*, (2) *long spoon*, (3) mid-spoon, (4) *short spoon*, (5) baffing-spoon, (6) driving-putter, (7) *putter*, (8) *sand-iron*, (9) *cleek*, (10) *niblick*, or track-iron. Those most useful in ordinary play are printed in italics: indeed, the ground must be very difficult and full of hazards to require them all.

These clubs – for they all come under that generic name – are put to a variety of uses. The play-club is used for swiping, or driving the ball off the tee at the commencement of a game.

If the ball rests on a hollow, amidst rough grass or on uneven ground, then the long spoon is used. The mid-spoon is used for the same purpose, for short distances only. When near the hole, the short spoon comes into play: indeed it and the shorter baffing-spoon are used to elevate the ball for short distances only. As the cleek answers the purpose of the latter, it is generally used in preference.

The putter is more like a club that the croquet-player would appreciate, for it comes into use when the ball lies on the putting-green within, say, eighteen or twenty yards of the hole.

If the player could insure the ball falling in pleasant green places, the foregoing clubs would suffice; but balls will fall at times in bunkers, as sand-holes are called, or fall in the whin-bushes, among the rushes and long bents, or among the rough stones of a road. Then the sand-iron is required.

The cleek is useful for driving balls over intervening obstacles lying between the ball and the hole near the putting-green. The niblick, sometimes called the track-iron, is used to drive the balls from deep hollows, cart-ruts, or from among the stiff coarse stems of the furze or whin-bushes.

On reaching your ball, if it lies on the open turf, you may repeat the long swipe with advantage if you are not too ambitious. If in a sand-hole, you will require your sand-iron; if in a hollow of the turf, the long spoon; if in a rut, the niblick. You will find the bunker, or sand-hole, a hazard to be avoided rather than courted. It will require patience and perseverance ere the ball can be driven from its snug retreat on to the turf at one stroke.

At length your ball lies on the green itself, and the hole is temptingly near. You now want judgment and nicety of touch. You have to consider, not only the distance between your ball and the hole, but the possibility of a stymie.

A stymie is an ugly affair for a beginner, and it occurs when your antagonist's ball lies in a direct line between your hole and the ball, so that putting is out of the question. There is no other course open but to take the sand-iron and 'loft' your ball over the stymie into the hole if you can. Stymies are sometimes played purposely, but it is not considered exactly fair to play them; but, whether played purposely or not, they often occur, and the young player should practise 'lofting' with a view to overcoming stymies when they occur. Even without this obstruction, he has to consider the necessary strength to drive his ball safely in. He must also consider the nature of the intervening ground, whether up-hill or otherwise, and the best way of overcoming the difficulty.

'To putt' well ought to be the aim of every beginner; and, as he can practise it on any greensward, it is his own fault if he does not succeed.

Anon, *The Game of Golf*, c 1870

THE FATHER OF GOLF: TOM MORRIS

This 15th day of June, 1891, appears to the writer a suitable one on which to take pen in hand, and scratch a few commonplaces about one of the best-known men in Scotland – Tom Morris. To expand him into Thomas Morris would be improper, a solecism to be looked for among the profane and vulgar, an equivalent to eating peas with a knife, or any other barbarity which shocks our refined sensibilities; to the brotherhood, therefore, let him be as he is, Tom Morris, or better still, the ever-popular favourite, Old Tom.

Tom's golfing career began at an early age. Being a native of St Andrews, his profession might, perhaps, have been anticipated, but as a matter of fact it was only determined by a haphazard remark of old Sandy Herd, who asked him why he did not get himself apprenticed to a club-maker. Negotiations with Allan Roberston followed, the upshot being that he took Tom into his employment, and taught him the trade with which his name has been identified for half a century. For our hero in good sooth is a man whom his warmest admirers would hardly characterise as a living embodiment of order and method.

Tom's name will ever be associated with the great match for £400 between Allan Roberston and himself against Willie and James Dunn, played in 1849. This match has been admirably described in a little book recently published by Mr Peter, who was an eye-witness. The match is ancient history, but the narrator invests it with such interest that one feels almost as if one were present to share the enthusiasm which animated the crowd. Tom and Allan were, to all intents and purposes, beaten, as much as twenty to one being laid on their opponents at a time when the latter were 4 ahead and 7 to play. But one after another these holes dropped off, till the match stood all square and 2 to play; but the penultimate hole must have been a trying one to the layers of the aforesaid odds. Allan and Tom had played three more, and were, besides, in a bunker; but the Dunns had come to grief at the back of a curb-stone on a cart track off the course.

Here they seem entirely to have lost all judgment, the last vanishing traces of which were indicated by a request on their part that a spade should be sent for and the rock of offence removed. When this was negatived by the umpire, they alternately kept missing the globe, by reason of the iron glancing off the stone,

Tom Morris Snr in full swing, 1899.

until one off three became the odds, when it occurred to them to play the ball out backhanded. Had they done this at first they must have won the hole, and, most probably, the match; instead of which they lost both. Mr Peter, it is satisfactory to see, records his opinion thus, 'I think it only just to say that, in my opinion, the winning of the above match was due to Tom Morris, who played with pluck and determination throughout.' Elsewhere he adds: 'Who has ever handled a club and does not know him, his genial countenance, dark, penetrating eye (his eye, however, is a blue-grey in colour), which never failed to detect a cunning road to the hole; imperturbable temper, unflinching courage, and indomitable self-control under circumstances the most exasperating.'

Tom has won the open championship four times, the scene of his victories being Prestwick on every occasion – in 1861, 1862, 1864 and 1867. His scores were 163, 163, 160 and 170, his most formidable antagonist being Park, who was never more than a stroke or two behind. On one occasion at Perth they tied at 168, but in playing off Tom won by fourteen strokes, Park being utterly at sea in the putting, which was very keen and difficult. Quite a unique feature in Tom's career is the extraordinarily fine game he has displayed almost continuously since his sixtieth year. Since then he has won two professional competitions, and on his sixty-fourth birthday holed St Andrews Links in 81, compiled with nothing above a five.

His services are in frequent request where new greens have to be exploited. Among those he has already laid out are Prestwick, Westward Ho! Luffness, Dornoch, Tain, Callander, Cheltenham, and the Honourable Company's new green at Muirfield.

Long may he live, this grand old golfer! All golfers may be proud of numbering Old Tom among their friends. His the native dignity which outweighs all factitious advantages; his the pleasant demeanour, courteous without servility, independent without aggression, which affects favourably to all, and renders the possessor the master of circumstances on every occasion. We may fitly conclude with an echo of the sentiment by Tom's favourite poet, page upon page of whom he delights in quoting:-

'The rank is but the guinea's stamp,
The man's the gowd for a' that.'

H. Everard, *Golf,* 1891

PART FOUR

A ROUND

OF GOLF

Introduction

Part of the pleasure of golf is its endless variety. Throughout the entire golfing globe, no two golf courses are alike, no two holes are alike and for the vast majority of part-time amateurs, no two swings are alike. In keeping with this theme, this section is a pot-pourri of elements including interesting items on the rising standard of ladies' golf, male golfers protesting against ladies' golf, the difficulties with finding a good caddy, the future of televised golf, as well as miscellaneous pieces on the game in general. While each deals with a different aspect of the sport, gathered together they reflect the strangely obsessional nature of golf and those who play it.

The 'endless variety' of golf courses: (Opposite) Fajara in The Gambia, (right) the dramatic 17th at the TPC, Sawgrass.

THE WEATHER

During the year 1910 the weather, our prophet says, will be on the whole peculiarly favourable for golf. January and February, especially in the northern portions of the world, will be in the main cold and disagreeable, and you must recall that if you cannot play golf where you are, it is also true that you cannot play where you are not, as for instance the Bermudas, you being in New York, for that is a manifest absurdity.

During March, owing to the fact that the zodiac starts in as it ought, the days will begin to get warmer and warmer, until, if everything goes well, the snow should be bravely vanishing away by the twenty-sixth. Our prophet is quite sure of the date.

In April and May the golf will be excellent. At times, to be sure, the rain will fall during your first or second rounds, but it will be dryer rain than usual, and nothing but the putting-greens will be wetted. June, July, August, and September have in all this year one hundred and twenty-two days, and our prophet predicts that one hundred and nine of them are going to be perfect for playing golf. Three out of the thirteen bad ones happen to be on Sundays, and the ten others will all come in a row. It is impossible, says our prophet, to determine exactly when.

September, 1910 will be uneven golfing, as a good deal of Scotch mist is scheduled. We advise you to lay in a store of warm clothing.

October more than makes up for its predecessor this year. It has thirty-one days to September's thirty, and the odd one is to be fair. You can safely play into November as late as the twenty-ninth, when the snow will fall about half-past eleven, turning about noon to a cold, bitter rain. December, unless you are where you are not, is, as usual, no good.

New Golfer's Almanac for the year 1910

EARLY DAYS OF TELEVISED GOLF

The televising of golf being a comparatively new business we have to pick it up as we go along. It is obviously far from perfect and I am hoping that readers of *Golf Illustrated* will give us the benefit of their comments on the matter. There are many questions on which those who 'looked in' at the Walker Cup may perhaps be willing to give us their personal opinions.

What are the parts, for instance, that they find most and least interesting? On returning from a three-hour sojourn at the top of the 60ft tower out by the Loop, completely perished with cold, I was handed a telegram on which some anonymous gentleman from Palmers Green had thought it worth while to spend three shillings, saying 'We want to see golf, not scenery.' If it is any consolation to him, I may add that this caused much innocent amusement in the Royal and Ancient at my expense – but does it represent the general view? I had another communication, signed this time, in the same strain, and I must say that both surprised me.

After all, we were portraying the most historic scene in golf, that wonderful panorama of the links at St Andrews with the 'old grey town' in the background, as never seen by human eye before except perhaps by low-flying pilots from Leuchars aerodrome, namely from a height of 60 ft. I thought it made a wonderful picture and that everyone, particularly those who have never been to the ancient shrine, would be interested to see it. It also seemed to me that the viewer at home, to whom we were to show the 11th green so many times, would feel more in the picture if from time to time we showed the 'backcloth', namely the Eden estuary. It may well be that this judgment was wrong. We can only tell if readers are kind enough to acquaint us with their opinions.

As to the commentary, which is my own main concern, another wire came from a Hunstanton viewer, who appeared satisfied with things in general but asked for the length of the holes to be given. This constructive criticism was much appreciated and will be noted for the future. I ought to have thought of it before. Again, do we talk too little or too much? For myself, I prefer to err on the side of what Sydney Smith described, in reference to the loquacious Macaulay, as 'brilliant flashes of silence', but there are plenty of asides about the players and their background with which one could perfectly well fill in the gaps if one knew that that was what people preferred.

For myself, I thought that the three solid hours allocated by the BBC on the Friday morning was a bit too much of a good thing but the official view seemed to be that people could always switch off if they wanted and that as all the apparatus was there it might just as well be used – and anyway, it was good practice.

The BBC have now laid a permanent cable at great cost out to the Loop so we may expect regular television from St Andrews henceforth, beginning with the Open in the first week in July. In the Walker Cup we were unfortunate in the foursomes landslide robbing Saturday's play of any dramatic interest. This is always liable to happen in match-play, in which in any case you cannot guarantee to show the climax, since it may take place far from the range of your cameras. The Open will be different. Unless we are very unlucky, we can be sure to show the winner actually winning and this, by the very slowness of it all, is to my mind one of the most dramatic scenes in sport. Here, the main television will come from the neighbourhood of the 18th green. All who remember the closing scenes at Birkdale last year will appreciate how exciting this may be.

If a television broadcast is successful, the commentator is liable to get the credit. The people who really ought to get it are those who are never seen, namely, the producer and the cameramen. At St Andrews the producer-in-chief was James Buchan, while Noble Wilson was in charge at the Loop in a tent jam-packed with equipment of quite extraordinary complexity. On top of the tower were the two cameramen whom I came to know, I am afraid, only as Bert and Andy, one of whom worked the 40in. lens which brings a man to fill the screen at a range of a quarter of a mile.

The producer in his tent cannot see the play. He can see on his screens what the cameras are showing now and can broadcast whichever he likes, but he cannot see what is going on elsewhere and what is the best thing to show next – and the cameramen cannot of course get on to it until he tells them where to go. The commentator can see, but, though he can hear in his earphones all the stage directions going on in the background, he cannot himself talk to the producer, except by breaking off the commentary to get the assistant to pass a message down on the separate telephone. Hence, the many rather palpable subterfuges such as 'I hope that when they have finished putting we shall be able to go across to the 8th and see Carr and Cherry who will just be ready to drive... etc.' All in all, therefore, it is no mean achievement on the part of the producer, sitting pretty well in darkness and able to see nothing whatever of the play, not only to show the present scene but at the same time to direct the other camera, together with precise directions as to the lens to be used, on to the next.

At one stage of the St Andrews proceedings a shot was shown, from the cameras by the 18th, of the general scene looking out over the course and including the tower from which I was myself talking. This was quite one of the queerest sensations I remember. By this extraordinary business of television one was actually looking at one's self from a range of a mile and a half!

All in all, I think the televising of golf has got off to a reasonable start, though, of course, there is room for improvement as we go along. I know that the official 'viewer reaction' to the Ryder Cup broadcast eighteen months ago showed a gratifying number of people who thought they would not be interested but in fact were, but my own main hopes are pinned on the Open, where, with continuous sports like Wimbledon and cricket going on at the same time, we shall be able to break into the afternoon's sporting programme only when we know that we have something dramatic to show – first, with luck, somebody setting up the target, as Syd Scott did at Birkdale, and then a succession of celebrities playing the last hole and trying to beat it. However, we shall see. In the meantime would any who have views on the Walker Cup broadcasts be so very kind as to let us have them?

Henry Longhurst, *Golf Illustrated* magazine, June 1955

A SUPERIOR SET OF MEN

It is your caddie's business to find out how far you drive with each club, and since a life-long experience will have taught him the exact relative position to the hole of

each blade of grass on the links, he ought to be always able to put into your hand the right club, almost without your asking for it. He will also know the idiosyncrasies of your play, to what extent he may allow you to 'greatly dare', out of what lie you may be permitted to play with a brassy, and all such little niceties.

Scottish professional Ben Sayers needing some help from his caddie at Prestwick, 1895.

Almost since he was born (in the year 1847) 'Fiery' has been connected with Golf, and it is a proof of his excellence as a caddie that young Willie Park has had him for helper in all his famous tournaments. He is one of those caddies who rank as high as the best professional, but who are purely carriers and coaches. 'Fiery' probably plays Golf, but not better than a second-class amateur. There is a batch of such men at Musselburgh. They are mostly very illiterate, but in their own way very respectable and deserving of respect.

My usual caddie, Flinn, is one of the same lot. He carries well, knows his employer's game, and almost never needs to be asked for a club – he has always the right one ready. His employer's clubs he keeps in good order. He is always sober during the day – at least, nearly always.

These men have no wish to do anything more than earn a living. Neither Flinn nor 'Fiery' attempt to sell balls, nor offer to remake them. They simply carry. They will have nothing to do with caddies who have ever been in gaol for theft, etc. Neither Flinn nor 'Fiery' would beg. They often starve. 'Fiery' is a very reticent man. No one knows more than that he is a bachelor, and lives in a lodging. No man ever saw him with his cap off, nor knows why he refuses to let his head be seen. He and his lot are quite heathens. They look on churches as for their betters, just as much as clubs. (This statement of Sir Walter's requires some qualification. Some of them, we happen to know, are good churchmen.) They would as soon expect to be invited to lunch in the one as to worship in the other.

I believe that in their own way 'Fiery' and his set are most reliable men... Whether 'Fiery' is better educated, or merely more intelligent, than most of his set I don't know; but he is a man of suave and polished manners. Yet he and two other caddies to whom we once gave a glass of champagne at St Andrews because we happened to have no whisky unpacked, all said they have never tasted wine before. 'Fiery' alone seemed to appreciate it. He disagreed with the others who did not wish to taste it again, and said he 'could see that men might come to like that, but for his part he did not think it had "eneuch o'grip"'.

Prints of William Gunn (Caddie Willie), a curious character of the golf links, are familiar in Scottish club-houses. One of the strangest peculiarities of this eccentric ancient caddie was the way in which he wore his clothes, and the extraordinary profile he presents in the prints of him is accountable to the fact that he continually carried his wardrobe on his back. All the clothes he got he put on his back, one suit above another. To admit of his wearing three or four coats at once, he had to cut out the sleeves to let them on. True to the uniform which invariably distinguished golfers in those days, an old red coat was always worn outside of them all. He also wore three or four vests, an old worn fur one being outermost. It was the same with his trousers – three or four pairs on, and the worst outermost; and three bonnets, sewed one within the other. He had his quarters at Bruntsfield, renting a garret.

Willie was very honest, paying his rent regularly, and for his bread and milk as he got it. He lived entirely on baps and milk, never having a warm diet or a fire in his garret, even in the coldest winter. 'Caddie Willie' was a Highlander, and could only speak English imperfectly. He was in the habit of tramping from Edinburgh to his Highland home every autumn when the golfing season closed. In 1820 he left Bruntsfield. From that journey poor Willie never returned, and all the inquiry golfers made never elicited his fate.

J. Kerr, *Golf*, 1893

SCHOOL ABSENTEES

(To) Harry Hart
Secretary Prestwick Golf Club

(From) Monkton & Prestwick School Board

Dear Sir,

School Absentees

As this matter has given this Board great anxiety and trouble, the Board has issued a circular to Parents, Guardians all with the view of inducing them to send children under their care to School with greater regularity.

The Board directed me to send you as Secretary of the Golf Club – the

J. Webb in a 1950s Artisans Championship at Wentworth, aided by his sons Tony (five) and Roger (three). Whether the boys were at school, and got permission for a day off, is not recorded.

accompanying copy for suspension in your club room and to request your committee's co-operation in this trying matter by seeing that boys between the ages of 5 and 14 who have not passed the fifth standard are not employed during school hours as caddies by your members!

Yours truly
Hugh Boyd Esq.
Clerk

Dated 25th Sept. 1891

THE SILENT CADDY

By this time Sandy Herd had been down at Hugh Philp's – then the only maker of Clubs in the place – rubbing up Whyte-Melville's irons. A bit of old emery-paper – the older the better as it did not scratch – was in the faithful caddie's hand, as he first rubbed along the blade, front and back, and then across at the point and heel of the face, so as to leave the centre with a different shade from the rest, that the eye might be more easily caught, when aiming at the ball in the wrist stroke or the long putt. He took a pride in having all the clubs nicely oiled with hare's foot (slightly dipped in linseed-oil, which hardly covered the bottom of an old tin can on the spare back bench of the shop.) A polish would thus be put on them 'like that on the back of an otter' – according to James Wilson's constant simile – and a 'skin' got on the handle, which made them weather any rain. Three days a week did the master take his 'two rounds'; and before he died the servant received a beautiful silver watch as a token of his faithfulness.

Sandy Pirie was also in Hugh's, getting ready Captain Maitland Dougall's instruments of war. Sandy had an idea that nobody could beat the Captain. No one ever saw Sandy try a shot himself; yet he knew every foot of the green, and every point of the Captain's play. He had the grand merit of *silence* during a match. He knew his master's mind by a sort of trained clairvoyance, and put into the Captain's hand the right club without being asked. Close behind he would faithfully follow, earnestly bent upon the match, carrying the clubs in his left hand, instead of the time-honoured method of carrying them within the left arm. On a passing player asking about the game, Sandy would remark 'We're twa ahint; but we'll mak' it up; we're no in oor play the day.' The 'we' showed the fidelity and interest of the old caddie.

Rev J. G. McPherson, *Golf and Golfers: Past & Present,* 1891

CADDY RATES

Musselburgh, 23rd September, 1834

It is resolved that the boys employed as Cadies shall be paid. For one round, Threepence; and for two or more Twopence each round. An engagement for the day not to exceed one shilling. Golfers from other places will see the propriety of giving effect to this resolution.

Minutes of the Musselburgh Golf Club

Inflation showing since 1834 as one man takes the enterprise economy to heart.

FORECADDIES AT BLACKHEATH

At Blackheath you require to have a forecaddie to run ahead with a red flag, and wave away nursemaids and perambulators, and such things, and you get lots of new experiences in the way of lamp-posts and benches and iron railings. The caddies, too, are a species to themselves, clad in long frock coats originally made for men about a foot taller than the present owners – all except one worthy of some 6 ft 3 ins in an Eton jacket. They have no sense of the fitness of things. The putting greens are not at all bad, and there are two of the longest holes I ever saw. Poor James, I felt quite sorry for him! The longest hole of all was in the teeth of a strong wind, and when James at length arrived at it he looked quite faint and pale, and said he felt as if he had been driving ever since he was a little boy.

Horace Hutchinson, *The Golfing Annual*, 1887-88

A HELPING HAND – OR FOOT

Undoubtedly, the strangest golf story of the year was last week's about John Montague of Los Angeles, who, after being recognised by Grantland Rice and other golf authorities as the most proficient player in the world, was recognised by the authorities of New York State as a suspect in a hold-up. The Montague epic – his mysterious appearance in California, his famous match against Bing Crosby, his ability to throw cards at the crack of a door or, when displeased, to hang his golfing competitors on the coat-racks in their lockers – has been too thoroughly recited in the Press for comment here. The whole affair, including Montague's shyness, which, now so explicable, was instantly and universally accepted, like Greta Garbo's, as the hall-mark of a rich personality, belongs to the true Hollywood tradition. It is only regrettable that the match, about which there were rumours last spring, between Montague and a top-notch Eastern amateur for $10,000 a side, now seems most unlikely to be played.

Golf seems to have a special fascination for characters whose careers belong to a world quite different from that of country clubs. None of them have achieved Montague's inconvenient excellence, but several have been notable at least for their eccentricity. Al Capone was not a particularly able golfer, but he played honestly and with enjoyment. The same compliment cannot be paid to the late Leo Flynn, who was a member of Jack Dempsey's board of strategy when Dempsey was the world's heavyweight champion. Amiable and engaging off the golf course, Flynn, who took up the game late in life and became a fanatical devotee, was irascible when playing, and though his scores were in the low seventies, he never had enough confidence in his ability to dispense with artificial aids. The most effective of these was a Negro caddie whom Flynn once hired by the month in Florida.

Friends noticed that the caddie always walked barefoot. It was his duty, when Flynn's ball went in the rough, to pick it up with his unusually long toes and, without stooping down, deposit it quietly on the fairway.

The most famous underworld golfer was, of course, Titanic Thompson, the gambler whose name was in the headlines for several weeks after the death of Arnold Rothstein. Thompson, who played left-handed, was sensationally good at golf, but even better at the side bets with which he always tried to brighten up a round. The most noteworthy example of Thompson's speciality was the thousand dollars he won when, pointing out a hound dozing on the fairway, he offered to bet his partner five to one that the dog would bark before either of them played their next shot. The instant after Thompson's friend took the bet, the dog barked – at a rabbit which Thompson, but not his companion, had seen running toward it through the long grass.

Despite Montague's glamorous reputation, the chances are that he is not the best golfer in the world. That title, if it belongs to anyone, belongs probably to Henry Cotton, who last week won the British Open Championship at Carnoustie. Not as well known in this country as some of his confrères who have played with Ryder Cup teams – which Cotton refused to join because he prefers to tour by himself – he is roughly the equivalent of a British Walter Hagen. Cotton's golf is more reliable, but a trace of the swaggering confidence that distinguished Hagen causes him to dress like a fashion plate, have a Swedish massage before important matches, and drive about in a roadster that looks as though it belonged on a speedway.

New Yorker, July 1937

ON CHOOSING A CADDY

Caddies are persons employed to carry golfers' clubs. Some people call them 'caudies', others try to do without them, but experience teaches that a bad one is better than none. On the older greens, where carrying is established as a free trade, there is a miscellaneous selection of caddies – boys, ragamuffins just out of prison, workmen out of a job, and professional carriers. All but the last ought to be avoided. A good boy to carry is not a bad thing in its way. From him too much must not be expected. If the tees he makes are not over two inches in diameter, if each time a club is required he is not further than three minutes walk from his master, if he knows the names of the clubs, he is a good boy. But on free greens when there are professionals, the boys do not come up to this standard. They are however, cheaper than professionals. The workman out of a job is not cheaper, besides being more inefficient than a boy.

From men who have adopted carrying as a trade the golfer is entitled to expect the highest standard of efficiency. If he carries for you regularly the professional

The caddy 'must never show the just contempt he has for your game'.

ought to know what club you intend to take, and to give it without being asked. When you are in doubt about how to play your shot, he ought to confirm you in the opinion you have formed regarding it. He must never show the just contempt he has for your game. Carrying clubs is one of the most agreeable trades open to the lower orders. In it an amount of drunkenness is tolerated which in any other would land the man in the workhouse. A very low standard of efficiency and very little work will secure a man a decent livelihood. If he is civil, willing to carry for three or four hours a day and not apt to drink to excess before his work is done, he will earn a fair wage, and yet be able to lie abed till nine in the morning like a lord. If he does not drink (this is a hard condition, as he has little else to do) he is positively well-off; if he makes balls and can play a good game himself, he may become rich. A caddy who in addition employs his leisure (of which there will still remain a great deal) in acquiring the elements of an education, may rise to be a green-keeper or a Club master, and after his death be better known to fame than many a defunct statesman or orator.

As a rule, however, the professional caddy is a contented being, spending what he gets as soon as he gets it, a Conservative in politics, a heathen in religion. He is a Conservative because he likes and admires gentlemen, who according to his idea, are the class which plays golf and overpays him. He is a heathen, churches being to his mind as sacred to gentlemen as Clubs.

Sir Walter Simpson, The Art of Golf, 1887

CADDY SIGN LANGUAGE

My first job was a fore-caddie, and I daresay it would be a couple of years before I was promoted to a carrying caddie. We used to get two shillings per day when acting as fore-caddie with a lunch at Mrs Forman's consisting of fourpence worth of bread and cheese. These were happy days, running as fore-caddies to mark down the ball as well as to show the line to the hole, for in those days there were no flags in the holes at Musselburgh. We had to learn to use a few simple signals to make the golfers acquainted with the kind of lie their shot had secured. They were very impatient, those old golfers; and as there was almost always a wager upon the match, you could not let them know too soon what their chances were of winning or losing the hole. If the ball landed in decent country, the fore-caddie had to face about towards the players and stroke his breast downward with his right hand. If the ball fell into whin or bunker, the mishap was telegraphed by a downward stroke of the right fist held out from the body. Two downward strokes conveyed the news that the lie was very bad indeed. A downward stroke and a gentle motion of the hand from right to left indicated that the ball was in the hazard but lying hopefully on a smooth surface. It was the duty of the fore-caddie when a ball fell among whins to mark the place with a piece of paper – which was liftable, of course, by the player – and then hurry on to take up a fresh stand.

Great Golfers in the Making, edited by Henry Leach, 1907

THE ABOLITION OF THE CADDIE

As in Ayr in 1899, there are crowds of caddies available at Lanna in Thailand. Here 15 of them accompany five players.

Most employers of labour in Ayr (says an Ayr correspondent of the 'Evening Times); complain of the dearth of boys either for office work, as apprentices to trades, or as messengers, and time and again they have expressed themselves to me regarding this paucity as a thing inexplicable, for, they invariably point out, are boys not in plenty, and to be seen loafing about in idleness at street corners or playing at cards on the Low Green? Yes, they are there all right, but they have had a spell at caddie work, and cannot settle down to staid employment thereafter. At the golf-houses from Ayr to Irvine they may be seen in crowds waiting for engagements. The work is congenial, and the 'chance' is good, and they spend days loafing on the links when they ought to be serving apprenticeships to useful

trades. There are hundreds and thousands of boys being sacrificed on the altar of golf, and the country made the poorer thereby. Were some of the players to carry their own clubs, I think they would find it almost as good exercise as the playing, and, methinks, the sheaf of sticks would grow beautifully less, and they would soon discover that they could do all that was necessary with four instruments.

Leamington Spa Advertiser, 1899

A POLITICAL PROBLEM

31st Dec 1923

Dear Mr Taylor,

I play little golf now since a crowd of yobs prevented my playing here (Lossiemouth) but I shall be so delighted to see you that I shall take up that challenge of yours. I am keeping your letter so as soon as I have a breathing space I shall arrange something. My handicap used to be 7 but I must now be something like 100. I shall take down a friend or two and we shall have a jolly day of it.

Yours very truly

Ramsay MacDonald

NO DIRECTIONS!

On a day in April, I walked round the Links with a 'foursome': the only time I ever did so. It is sad to make such a confession: but truth must be told. My brother Alexander and Lord Colin Campbell played against Tulloch and a golfer departed. It was extraordinary how peppery the golfers became. Tulloch and his partner were being badly beaten, and became demoralised. Tulloch, seeing his partner doing something stupid, made some suggestion to him. On which his irate friend brandished his club in the air, and literally yelled out, 'No directions! I'll take no directions!' Tulloch used to complain that an old story of the Links and their provocations, applicable to another Principal, had come to be told of him. 'How is the Principal getting on with his game?' was asked of one of the caddies of a returning party. 'Ah!' said the caddie, with an awestricken face, 'he's tappin' his ba's, and dammin' awfu'.'

A. H. K. Boyd, *Twenty-Five Years of St Andrews*, 1892

A WORM'S PARADISE

'We believe that to charge as most clubs do three or four guineas entrance and a like subscription is ridiculous and unreasonable, and that there are scores of would-be golfers who are prevented from playing on the grounds of expense alone.'

These are the remarks made by the chairman at a meeting called for the purpose of forming a golf club, and the meeting decided that, as 46 ladies and gentlemen had promised to become members, they would form a club, and before the meeting broke up they agreed that the entrance fee and subscription should be one guinea. They had already selected the ground on which to lay out a nine-hole course, and a committee was formed to enter into negotiations with the farmer.

Now, without wishing to damp the enthusiasm of these good people, I am of opinion that they are asking for trouble. They evidently know very little of the expenses connected with the making of a golf course, even on a modest scale. I know the ground that they propose to rent, and at the outset they are up against a stiff proposition in the person of the farmer. This same son of the soil had formerly let a portion of his land to a club, but had he persisted in turning his cattle in, to the detriment of the greens, they had no choice but to shift their quarters. The professional who was attached to this club has related to me the story of how on one occasion he turned the cattle off the links. This coming to the ears of the farmer brought him on the scene with a loaded gun. The timely warning of a caddie probably saved the pro's life, for when he arrived at the clubhouse the pro was nowhere to be found.

However small the club is, a nine-hole course cannot be brought into play under an expenditure of £250. The cost of labour, horse hire, machines, etc., would soon swallow up this amount, and there is always something required even when the committee think everything is in order. There are few, if any, courses that are as they were originally laid out, for it is not until they are played over that faults appear, and then begins the real work on a course. This bunker is in the wrong place, and that tee is dangerous, or it may be that more bunkers are necessary.

For a club with a membership of 200, possessing an eighteen-hole course, the subscription should be at least three guineas, for it is not possible to keep everything as it should be with a less sum, and when a club is formed the members should realise this, and not fix the entrance fee at a guinea as an inducement for others to join, for sooner or later they will awake to the fact that good golf cannot be obtained at this price, and if they do manage to rub along and keep the right side of the balance-sheet, the result will be seen in the condition of the course.

B. Radford, *Golfing*, 1910

'In golf, whilst there is life there is hope.' A 1930s seaside golfer demonstrates the truth of that statement.

NEVER DESPAIR OF GOLF

Golf is not one of those occupations in which you soon learn your level. There is no shape nor size of body, no awkwardness nor ungainliness, which puts good golf beyond one's reach. There are good golfers with spectacles, with one eye, with one leg, even with one arm. None but the absolute blind need despair. It is not the youthful tyro alone who has cause to hope. Beginners in middle age have become great, and more wonderful still, after years of patient duffering, there may be a rift in the clouds. Some pet vice which has been clung to as a virtue may be abandoned, and the fifth-class player burst upon the world as a medal winner. In golf, whilst there is life there is hope.

Sir Walter Simpson, *The Art of Golf*, 1887

IN PRAISE OF WOMEN'S GOLF

The great desideratum of the age appears to be a game for ladies, which will combine a sufficient amount of exercise with that gracefulness of deportment which every true woman is properly proud of possessing. *Grace and women* should

An aspiring Edwardian actress with her golf clubs, proving that 'both grace and comeliness will be her portion'.

be synonymous, for were it not for the refining influence and the beauty and elegance of the women, what a coarse, rude, and ugly world this would soon become. A world without women would be worse than a world without flowers, and therefore it is every woman's duty to cultivate grace and comeliness. Let her play Golf to her heart's content, being assured that both grace and comeliness will be her portion.

Letter to the Editor of Golf Magazine, February 1891

LADY GOLFERS

The lady golfer is a distinct genus, belonging to the order of Amazonæ, or athletic women. Interesting and instructive are the characteristics of the species, pity space prohibits a detailed account of its acquired and inherited habits; they are, however, very obvious to the *eruditi* in girls' games and sports. Lady golfers are found at every age, in all parts of the world. With curls down their backs, in abbreviated skirts, we meet them flying over the Shinnecock Hills, U.S.A., or silverhaired, bespectacled, bonneted, they waggle on the Wimbledon Common! Amid the desert near Bagdad they hole-out, win championships in New Zealand, and tea at the neat chalet pavilion on the top of the Mustapha slopes, Algiers. Their chief habitat is the United Kingdom; here they possess over one hundred and twenty clubs, of which nearly all have been instituted since the eighties. The evolution of the lady player may be studied by those who have no acquaintance with fossils or comparative anatomy. We trace her descent through Mary Queen of Scots, to the fishwives of Musselburgh. On the principle that a Norman ancestor is more usually quoted than a Victorian greengrocer grandmamma, the fact of Mary having played in the fields round Seton is better known than the instance of the fish ladies' competition in 1810 for a new Barcelona handkerchief, a new creel, and shawl. Although we cannot determine the exact sequence of women drivers and putters who preceded Queen Mary into the remotest hazards of history, we have those records of their near relative – the male player – which guide us in the right direction; for it would not be possible that Scotch father, brother, and husband should play the game during many hundred years without their women folk joining in foursomes, or engaging among themselves in terrible single combat. Indeed, it may be proved that the discovery of golf was due to a woman. The pre-historic shepherd who hit a pebble with his crook into a neighbouring rabbit-hole, and thus accidentally originated the game, did so in a fit of ill-humour that his shepherdess was late for the *rendez-vous!*

The reason of woman's tardy introduction on Southron greens is that her presence there was somewhat severely interdicted in the Badminton book: firstly, lest men should find it hard to decide between flirting and playing the game;

In the 1890s 'the volubility of female tongue and skirt' may have been considered a problem by some men. A hundred years later, Danielle Cromb makes sure that no one could object to her skirt being too voluble.

secondly, because of the volubility of female tongue and skirt; and thirdly, that should she volunteer to score there could be no manner of doubt in whose favour she would do so! However, as women grew more independent in their habits, and cultivated a love of fresh air and sport, lady golfers became naturalised in England, and notwithstanding a length of prize list and a shortness of course, factors not favourable to the production of first-class play, attention to style, keenness, and practice have developed within the last five years a game which elicits high praise in all parts where their championship has been held. Critical, able judges pronounce the drive of our best players to be both long and straight, their approach a matter of surprise, their putting more cool and accurate than men's.

Lady golfers may be classed under three heads, and treated of individually, viz.: the Golfer, scratch or handicap, the Pot-Hunter, the Player. *The Golfer* is often one of the younger and latest members of the club. A good match and a good score are her pleasures. She takes a genuine interest in links and clubs. From her the

secretary hears no complaints of the difficulties on the course or the unfairness of *In the early 1880s* her luck. She is a favourite with the handicap committee, because a reduction of her *golf was considered* odds is followed by no outcry; it dares curtail her allowance on any improvement of *an unsuitable pastime* form shown, not waiting for a win; her ambition being a championship, not a button- *for ladies, so they were* hook! *The Pot-Hunter* – These professional prize-catchers are fortunately not common, *restricted to a small* but most of us have had the opportunity of studying their habits. Their only *putting green to the* enjoyment is in winning. They are no sportswomen. If they lose, we know that we *right of the first hole* shall all hear about their bad luck. The way that bad luck 'goes' for them is *on the Old Course at* extraordinary. According to them, lies are infinitely worse in the particular spot *St Andrews. By* where their ball rests than anywhere else on the links, even in the bunkers! The *1890, however,* hazards seem to get up and follow them round the course! They have never been *women golfers could* properly handicapped, yet most of them have played a long time and belong to *be found on almost* many clubs. The fashion of undervaluing one's own powers, especially when *every course in* accompanied by an over-appreciation of those of others, is so unusual in life that *Scotland.* when we find it on the links we may confidently assert that such modesty is incompatible with morality. Pot-Hunters never seem to have any game of their own to think about, but they make up for this by taking a five-hundred horse-power interest in other people's. *The Player* – Happy, light-hearted, irresponsible players! All serious golfers love you. Sparkling, gaseous, bright, an effervescence of youth and amusement. We recognise you by your fluttering pretty dress, merry laughter, irrelevant movements. You hurry out to the tee, and rush back again for balls! You putt and talk with the flag in the hole; and add up the score on the green while two cracks wait to play their approach. Such incidents as stymies, honours, penalty strokes, you take no note of. When after a round, where we have seen you and your caddies walking *off* instead of on the course, with a handsome allowance of twenty-four you win an enamelled brooch, we are pleased and congratulate you. We do not even expostulate when, on the point of striking off the tee, we are suddenly startled and miss the globe by hearing eager voices discuss Mrs B.'s last dance from an adjacent green. No! We glance at the bright young faces so unconscious of the enormity of that offence which has cost us our record round, and – forgive. Healing influence of youth and good spirits! Desert not our links for the lawn-tennis courts and hockey-fields. To preserve you we will cede the golfers' unwritten rule of silence. Talk on, therefore, unrebuked. For you are always talking as fast as you can. Casual observers might think you had nothing to do with the game, and had merely come out for two hours' hard conversational exercise! Nevertheless we like you. You are not always in trouble, neither do you worry about other people's handicaps.

Amy Bennet Pascoe, *Golf and Golfers*, 1899

OBLIVIOUS

Accordingly just as the Colonel after a short walk returns to his ball, Miss Wilkinson answers Gurney's observation; so the Colonel misses his stroke and much grumbling about the irregularity of females appearing on the links is imperfectly overheard. The ladies are still pleasingly unconscious of the Colonel's wrath, and instead of gracefully withdrawing begin to take an interest in the game and ask Gurney questions about it, which he answers in a timorous and abrupt manner, justly dreading another outbreak on the part of his irascible opponent.

H.J.M. *The Cornhill Magazine*, April, 1867

LADIES' LINKS

We therefore gladly welcomed the establishment of ladies' links – a kind of Jews' quarter – which have now been generously provided for them on most of the larger greens. Ladies' links should be laid out on the model, though on a smaller scale, of the 'long round'; containing some short putting holes, some longer holes, admitting of a drive or two of seventy or eighty yards, and a few suitable hazards. We venture to suggest seventy or eighty yards as the average limit of a drive advisedly, not because we doubt that cannot well be done without raising the club above the shoulder. Now, we do not presume to dictate, but we must observe that the posture and gestures requisite for a full swing are not particularly graceful when the player is clad in female dress.

Lord Moncreiff, *Golf*, The Badminton Library, 1890

Laura Davies, the most successful woman professional of her generation, showing power and balance during impact.

DISTRACTED BY SHADOWS

It is to their presence as spectators that the most serious objection must be taken. If they could abstain from talking while you are playing, and if the shadow of their dresses would not flicker on the putting green while you are holing out, other objections might perhaps be waived...

If they volunteer to score, they may, and probably will score wrong (not in your favour you may be sure); yet you cannot contradict them. An outraged golfer once said to his opponent in a single who had brought his wife to score for him three days in succession, 'My good fellow, suppose we both did it!' This was in the circumstances a very strong and cogent way of putting the case; because there was no manner of doubt what the speaker's wife would do if she came. But the remonstrance was not well received and the match was not renewed.

Lord Moncreiff, Golf, Badminton Library, 1890

IT'LL NEVER LAST

North Berwick,
9th April, 1893

Dear Miss Martin,

I have read your letter about the proposed Ladies' Golf Union with much interest. Let me give you the famous advice of Mr Punch (since you honour me by asking for my opinion). *Don't*. My reasons? Well!

(1) Women never have and never can unite to push any scheme to success. They are bound to fall out and quarrel on the smallest or no provocation; they are built that way!

(2) They will never go through one Ladies' Championship with credit. Tears will bedew, if wigs do not bestrew, the green.

OPPOSITE PAGE:
'Constitutionally and physically women are unfitted for golf.' By 1903 in Torquay, women were already disproving this statement.

(3) Constitutionally and physically women are unfitted for golf. They will never last through two rounds of a long course in a day. Nor can they ever hope to defy the wind and weather encountered on our best links even in spring and summer. Temperamentally the strain will be too great for them. *The first Ladies' Championship will be the last*, unless I and others are greatly mistaken. The L.G.U. seems scarcely worth while...

AN IMPROBABLE STORY

I have seen a golfing novel indeed; but it was in the manuscript, the publishers having rejected it. The scene was St Andrews. He was a soldier, a statesman, an orator, but only a seventh-class golfer. She being St Andrews-born, naturally preferred a rising player. Whichever of the two made the best medal score was to have her hand. The soldier employed a lad to kick his adversary's ball into bunkers, to tramp it into mud, to lose it, and he won; but the lady golfer would not give her hand to a score of 130. Six months passed, during which the soldier studied the game morning, noon and night, but to little purpose. Next medal-day arrived, and he was face to face with the fact that his golf unbacked by his statesmanship, would avail him nothing. He hired and disguised a professional in his own clothes. The ruse was successful; but alas! The professional broke down. The soldier disguised as a marker, however, cheated and brought him in with 83. A three for the long hole roused suspicion and led to enquiry. He was found out, dismissed from the club, rejected by the lady (who afterwards made an unhappy

Opera singer Harry Death wasn't trying to disguise himself in a suit of armour, but to win a wager. He lasted the course at Ruislip, but sadly lost the match 2 and 1.

marriage with a left-handed player) and sent back in disgrace to his statesmanship and oratory. It was as good a romance as could be made on the subject, but very improbable.

Sir Walter Simpson, *The Art of Golf*, 1887

A REVIEW OF THE FUTURE

We have no wish to be unnecessarily harsh in our estimate of this book by J.A.C.K., – *Golf in the Year 2,000, or What We Are Coming To* – for whose excursion into literary pastures, as he tells us in the preface, himself shall hardly account, still, candour compels the admission that J.A.C.K., if the unpleasant pleasantry be allowed to pass, is not exactly a 'ripper' in the arts and graces of authorship.

Like Rip Van Winkle, the narrator falls into a trance, and sleeps for a hundred and eight years, at the end of which time he awakes to find, not unnaturally, that he and his surroundings have 'suffered a sea change'.

Several wonderful things happen; shaving has been improved out of existence, in lieu thereof a magical depilatory removes the beard by touch; when dinner time arrives the table is found to be 'made of three concentric circular pieces, and the middle one sank down through the floor, leaving intact the outer one, which formed the edge of the complete table'; 'the dumb waiter portion reappeared, bearing two plates of soup on it'.

The Chief Inspector when the time arrives for serious business, gives his guest the choice of a green on which to have a match; 'They are all equally convenient, from Thurso to Penzance; if you cared, we could even play a round on both of the greens I have mentioned.' So by means of an electric tubular railway, they find themselves at St Andrews almost before they have time to wink. Arrived there, it is necessary to procure a set of clubs, and a golfing coat, this latter a garment which subsequently develops unexpected, not to say alarming qualities. The starting is managed by phonograph, in conjunction with a board outside the window, on which board every man's name appears when his turn arrives. It is satisfactory to find that due sense of order and decorum prevails; in fact, no one is at the tee but the opponent.

The vagrom schoolboy, if under the age of fifteen, has no place in this economy, nor are there any caddies – none in the flesh, that is to say. As substitutes there are perpendicular rods about four feet high, weighted at the foot and hung upon wheels, the magnetic qualities of the employer's golfing jacket serving to keep them in tow, at a respectful distance of twelve feet. The clubs have advanced with the age, and are fitted with a dial apparatus for automatically registering every shot played, for there is a competition every day, and 'we have got handicapping as near perfection as possible, for we have a record of every round a man plays, and by taking his average from day to day and from week to week, we soon arrive at this right figure.'

Another automatic apparatus registers the length of every carry; the thickness of the grip can be altered at will in a moment, and the shape of the clubs, all made of steel in one piece, is such that they can be used either right or left-handed. The niblick is a work of genius; when swung over the shoulder its queerly-shaped double head begins to revolve on its own account with exceeding velocity, like a paddle-wheel, only faster, and ejects out of the bunker clouds of sand sufficient to keep 'Old Tom's' greens going for a twelvemonth. Moreover, the golfing jacket shouts 'Fore' every time a drive is made, to the detriment, until one becomes habituated to it, both of the stroke and of the temper.

Not without a touch of humour does the author allow his imagination free play in dealing with the future of the game, when match play shall have been almost improved out of existence, and the self-acting putter does everything short of telling you the line of your putt. The pity of it is that the ideas are clothed in such slip-shod English, grating on one at every turn, itself sufficient to mar the effect of the whole, however rich the imagination, or amusingly extravagant the general conception.

Golf, 1892

A SHORT ESSAY BY 'AN DUN'

Some years ago when snow lay in the glens and the greens were hard as rocks, I putted out of bounds. As the little mite sped across the frosted turf and disappeared beneath the frozen river that lay in silent wait beyond, a decision was born that as quickly became resolve. I would forsake the game for ever (or at least until the spring) and turn instead to books.

This raised the question: why do we browse, collect, read and generally delight in bibliomania, and why particularly in the literature of a sport called golf? Maybe it is for instruction – 'if all else fails read the instructions'; or we may seek entertainment – to enjoy the thought without being disappointed by the deed; perhaps it is for amusement – to savour the riches enshrined in the funny things of life; or we may find vicarious pleasure – rejoicing a touch when reading of the victor as (s)he smilingly bestrides the final fairway or castigating the daftness of a loser as (s)he fluffed the final chip.

Conceivably, it is knowledge we pursue – by absorbing the history and traditions of the game enjoyment is heightened and wisdom born – vision, after all, depends on the ability to interpret what is seen; again, we may just love the feel and smell and touch of well-bound paper, the craft and art that goes into the making of a good book, the consummate thrill of identifying fresh editions, locating hidden bargains and unearthing unsuspected titles; a few of us, if we are honest, collect because that is our obsession; to find, record, possess and ever wallow in unending search.

Another thought assails me. Some of us may nourish a secret interest in finance, reasoning to ourselves (and maybe to our spouses and bank managers as well) that every dollar spent on literature is actually an investment, a hedge against inflation or the need for a latter-day pension. For, when all is said and done, as the saloon keeper in north-west cattle country said during a blizzard, 'Cheer up boys, whatever happens to the cattle, the books won't freeze' – unlike that green of mine of long ago!

An Dun, *A Short Essay*, 1995

A rare photograph, taken in Perth in 1864, of a group of early Scottish professionals, including Tom Morris Jnr (back row, second left) and Tom Morris Snr, to his right.

ACKNOWLEDGEMENTS

A.A. Milne. 'The Great Secret' from *Not that it Matters*, © A.A. Milne, 1919. Reproduced by permission of Curtis Brown, London.

R.C. Robertson. 'Strange Opponents and Partners' from *Glasgow Morning Post*, 1935.

Arnold Haultain. The Mystery of Golf, Norwood Press, Mass., USA, 1910.

Stephen Potter. 'Golf Gamesmanship' from *The Complete Golf Gamesmanship* (Heinemann, 1968), © Stephen Potter, 1968

P.G. Wodehouse. 'Mortimer Sturgis' from *Ordeal by Golf*, (Omnibus of Golf Stories, 1973). Reprinted by permission of A.P. Watt Ltd.

A.C.M. Croome. 'Oxford Golf' from *The Royal & Ancient Game of Golf*, 1912. Published by London & Counties Press Association, reproduced courtesy of *Golf Weekly*.

Frank C. Tone 'Warding off a Brainstorm' from *The American Magazine*, 1928.

H.H. Hilton. 'Balance not Beauty' from *The Royal & Ancient Game of Golf*, 1912. Published by London & Counties Press Association, reproduced courtesy of *Golf Weekly*.

Horace Hutchinson. 'Indian Officers' from *Fifty Years of Golf*, Country Life Library, 1914.

Horace Hutchinson. 'Westward Ho!' from *The Midland Golfer*, 1913.

Eddie Loos. 'The Eight-Inch Golf Course' from *American Golfer magazine*, 1922.

Garden G. Smith. 'Temperament in Golf', 'Justice in Golf', 'The Early Links', 'The Golfers Garb' and 'The Social Side' all from *The Royal & Ancient Game of Golf*, 1912. Published by London & Counties Press Association, reproduced courtesy of *Golf Weekly*.

Bobby Jones. 'Playing the Road' from *Bobby Jones on Golf*, 1931, One-time Publishers, New York.

H. B. Martin. 'Bobby Jones' from *50 Years of American Golf*, 1936, Dodd Mead Ltd, New York.

Dale Concannon. 'The Making of The Masters' from *Golf: The Early Days*, Salamander Books, 1995. Reprinted by permission of the author.

Audrey Howell. 'The Dream Begins' from *Harry Vardon: The Revealing Story of a Champion Golfer*, © Stanley Paul & Co, 1991.

Michael Hobbs. 'Seve Ballesteros' and 'Nick Faldo' both from *British Open Champions*, Chapmans Library of Golf, 1991. Reproduced by permission of the author.

Bernard Darwin. 'A Stage for Leading Ladies' from *Green Memories*, 1928. Permission by A.P. Watt Ltd on behalf of Ursula Mommens, Lady Darwin & Dr Paul Ashton.

Bernard Darwin. 'The Triumvirate' from *Out of the Rough*, 1932. Permission by A.P. Watt Ltd on behalf of Ursula Mommens, Lady Darwin & Dr Paul Ashton.

David Davies. 'Woosnam Wins the US Masters', © *Guardian* 8 April 1992. Reproduced by permission of the author.

Henry Longhurst. 'Early Days of Televised Golf' from *Golf Illustrated*, June 1955. Reproduced courtesy of Golf Weekly.

'An Dun', 'A Short Essay'. Reproduced with permission of the author, 1995.

H.G. Whigham. 'The Common Sense of Golf' from *The American Golfer*, 1910.

J.C. Law. 'Driving to Destruction' from *The Irish Golfer*, 1902.

John L. Low. 'How to go about buying a putter' from *Concerning Golf*, 1903. Reproduced by permission of Hodder and Stoughton Ltd.

John L. Low. 'The Endless Variety of Golf' and 'Golf and the Man' both from *The Royal & Ancient Game of Golf*, 1912. Published by London & Counties Press Association, reproduced courtesy of *Golf Weekly*.

While every effort has been made by the author and the publishers to trace copyright holders, in some cases this has not been possible. They apologise to those whose names may have been inadvertently omitted.

All photographs in this book, unless otherwise credited, are from the Phil Sheldon Golf Picture Library, the archive photographs are from the Dale Concannon Golf History Collection at the Phil Sheldon Golf Picture Library.

The author would like to offer his grateful thanks to the following: Ian Marshall of Headline Book Publishing; Phil Sheldon; Gill Sheldon; Richard Collins of Salamander Books; Archie Baird, Gentleman Golfer of Gullane; Michael Hobbs; Christina Steinmann; Rhod McEwan; David Kirkwood; David Cannon; Jenny Davies of Hodder & Stoughton Ltd; Allsport; Christie's Images; Jim Colville; Curtis Brown Ltd; David Lea; Longman Group UK Ltd; Bob Waters of *Golf Weekly*; Corbis UK; Sotheby's Press Department; David Davies; Nick Potter of Burlington Galleries; William A. Roberto; Walter Mechilli; David Cronin; Tim Ward; Robert Aziz; John Sinnot; Rosemary Anstey; Bill Brett; John Joinson of Phillips, Chester; Simon Trewin of Sheil Land Associates; and the innumerable private golf collectors for their help and assistance, and especially Joseph Tiscornia, current holder of the Grand Match Medal.